HARD-DISK MANAGEMENT

THE POCKET REFERENCE

Kris Jamsa

Osborne **McGraw-Hill**
Berkeley, California

Osborne **McGraw-Hill**
2600 Tenth Street
Berkeley, California 94710
U.S.A.

For information on translations and book distributors outside of the
U.S.A., please write to Osborne **McGraw-Hill** at the above address.

IBM is a registered trademark of IBM Corp.

Hard-Disk Management: The Pocket Reference

1234567890 DODO 898

ISBN 0-07-881480-4

Acquisitions Editor: Cindy Hudson
Copy Editor: Kay Luthin
Word Processor: Bonnie Bozorg
Proofreader: Juliette Anjos
Technical Illustration/Page Composition: Peter Hancik
Production Supervisor: Kevin Shafer

CONTENTS

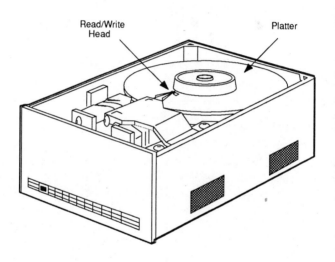

Read/Write Head

Platter

▶ INTRODUCTION

This pocket reference is a convenient guide if you currently own a hard disk or if you are thinking of purchasing one. Just about the only item for which sales have kept pace with the personal computer over the past few years is the hard (or fixed) disk. Most systems today are shipped with a minimum of a 20- or 30- megabyte disk.

Because of their tremendous speed and storage potential, hard disks require more user management than do floppy disks. As a result, the market is full of books that discuss hard disks. Unfortunately, most of these books simply discuss DOS. This pocket reference, on the other hand, discusses all of the factors that you will need to know to get up and running with your hard disk. It also tells you how to maximize your hard disk's performance and organization. In short, it tells you how to get the most from your hard disk.

▶ WHAT IS A HARD DISK?

Since the introduction of the IBM PC in 1981, the IBM PC and PC compatibles have dropped in price from several thousand dollars to, in some cases, several hundred. Until recently, the most common system configuration for a PC was a dual-floppy-disk system with drives A and B, as shown here:

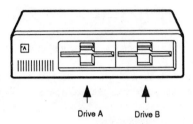

Drive A   Drive B

For many years, users found that dual floppy disks were more than adequate for storing programs and data for simple word-processing and spreadsheet needs. However, just as personal computer technology has increased over the past few years, so too has the complexity of user applications. PCs are now common fixtures in offices. In addition, many workers have realized the tremendous flexibility that having a PC at home can add to their lives. Thus, user applications are outgrowing the space limitations of floppy disks, and many users are migrating to a faster disk that provides tremendous storage capabilities: a hard disk.

If you have computer experience, you are probably familiar with standard 5 1/4-inch floppy disks. These are called *removable storage media* because you insert the floppy disk into a disk drive when you need the information that the disk contains, and you later remove the disk from the drive when it is no longer required:

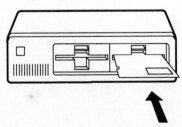

Unlike removable floppy disks, hard disks are fixed to your computer's chassis. Unless you physically disconnect the drive and remove it from your computer, a hard disk is always present in your system, as shown here:

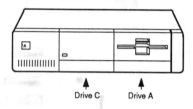

Drive C   Drive A

Some manufacturers of special hard disks, such as the Bernoulli disk, allow you to remove the disk and transport it to a different system or place it in a safe for storage. However, since these disks are not as common as the built-in hard disk, this reference will not discuss their use.

Although most systems in the future will be shipped with a single floppy-disk drive and a hard disk, depending upon your requirements, your system can still have two floppy-disk drives (A and B) in addition to a hard disk (drive C), as shown here:

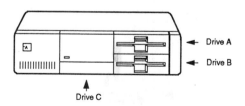

Drive A
Drive B
Drive C

A hard disk's advantage over a floppy disk is its speed and tremendous storage capacity. To understand how a hard disk is faster than a floppy disk, consider how your disk drive retrieves information stored on the disk. If you examine a floppy disk, you will find a small oval opening at the bottom of the disk, called the *read/write opening:*

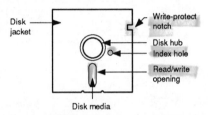

Disk jacket — Write-protect notch — Disk hub — Index hole — Read/write opening — Disk media

Once you insert the floppy disk into a disk drive, the disk begins spinning within the drive so that the entire surface of the disk is eventually exposed through the small read/write opening.

Within the drive a mechanism called the *read/write head* stores and retrieves information from the disk:

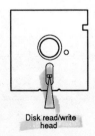

Disk read/write head

When DOS needs to read information from a file, the drive keeps track of the spinning disk until it reaches the beginning of the file. The drive then reads the information that the file contains as the disk rotates past the read/write head. A floppy disk spins within the drive at a rate of about 300 revolutions a minute.

Unlike floppy-disk media, which is plastic and therefore flexible, hard disks are solid. As a result, hard disks can spin much faster than can floppy disks, reaching speeds of up to 3600 revolutions a minute. Since the hard disk is spinning so rapidly, your disk drive is able to locate and manipulate information on the disk much faster than it can from a floppy disk.

The amount of time that it normally takes your disk drive to locate information on disk is called the *access time*. Access time is normally measured in thousandths of a second (milliseconds). The lower the access time, the faster your disk. If you are considering purchasing a hard disk, compare the access times as well as price. If you are saving considerable money, you are probably sacrificing access time. In most cases, the amount of time a faster disk saves you will, in the end, more than make up for its additional cost.

The second major advantage that hard disks provide you is tremendous storage capacity. Depending upon your specific disk type, a floppy disk can range in storage from 360 kilobytes (368,640 bytes) to 1.2 megabytes (1,228,800 bytes). In a similar manner, your hard disk can range in size from 10 megabytes (or 10 million bytes) to several hundred million bytes.

Don't be confused by the term *byte*. A byte is roughly equivalent to a character of information, so if your disk can store 368,640 bytes, it can store 368,640 characters. To better understand this value, consider a typed single-spaced page, which contains about 4000 characters (or bytes). A 360K (kilobyte) floppy disk can store about 90 of these pages. A 10MB (megabyte) hard disk, on the other hand, can store almost 2700 pages. The following table contrasts the number of floppy disks that it takes to equal the storage capacity of 10- and 20-megabyte hard disks:

Hard Disk	Equivalent Number of Floppy Disks
10MB	29 double-sided, double-density, 360K floppies
10MB	9 quad-density, 1.2MB floppies
20MB	58 double-sided, double-density, 360K floppies
20MB	18 quad-density, 1.2MB floppies

To understand why your hard disk can store more information than a floppy, you must understand how DOS stores information on your disk. First examine how DOS stores information on a floppy disk. DOS divides your disk into several concentric rings, called *tracks*. These tracks are similar to the grooves in a record album:

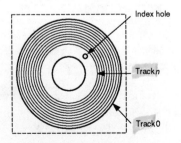

Index hole

Track *n*

Track 0

DOS divides each track into 512-byte storage locations, called *sectors:*

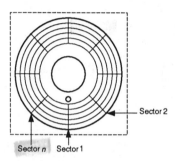

Depending on your disk density (the number of sectors per track and tracks per side), the amount of information that your disk can store will differ:

Disk Type	Number of Tracks	Number of Sectors
360K	40	9
720K	80	9
1.22MB	80	15
1.44MB	80	18
10MB	306	17
20MB	615	17

To determine the specific amount of information that your disk can store, use the equation

Storage capacity = (number of sides) * (number of tracks) * (sectors per track) * (bytes per sector)

13

In the case of a 360K floppy disk, for example, the equation becomes

Storage capacity = 2 * 40 * 9 * 512
= 368,640 bytes

Unlike floppy disks, which have a single disk for storage, hard disks are composed of two or more storage disks, called *platters:*

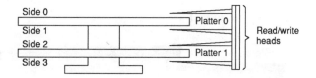

Thus, a 10-megabyte disk has four sides on which to store information, as opposed to two sides on a floppy disk. In addition, hard disks normally have 17 sectors per track, with more tracks per side. (Most discussions about hard disks refer to tracks as *cylinders;* the terms for our use are interchangeable.) A 10-megabyte disk, for example, uses 306 tracks per side; a 20-megabyte disk uses 615. Using this information, you can determine the exact storage capacity of a 10-megabyte disk as follows:

Storage capacity = 4 * 306 * 17 * 512
= 10,653,696 bytes

As you have just learned, your hard disk's hardware allows it to store more information than your floppy disk, while decreasing the amount of time it takes the disk to retrieve information. As you will learn later in this reference, there is another advantage offered by a hard disk. By placing all of your files on one disk, you can improve your file organization by reducing the number of disks that contain duplicate files, as well as reducing the number of disks that you must keep track of.

▶ PURCHASING A HARD DISK

Once you decide to purchase a hard disk, there are several factors that you should consider.

- What are your storage requirements?

- What are your speed requirements?

- What are the current applications that you want to place on the hard disk?

- Where can you obtain the fairest price?

- Who is going to perform the installation?

- What is the warranty?

- Where can you get the disk replaced or repaired?

The size of a hard disk can vary from ten megabytes to several hundred megabytes. To determine the size of the hard disk that you require, make a list of the applications you mean to place on your hard disk, along with the number of floppy disks that the applications currently requires.

Word processing	1	360K disk
Spreadsheet	4	360K disks
Database	4	360K disks
DOS	2	360K disks
Desktop publishing	9	360K disks
MS Windows	6	360K disks
Total	26	360K disks

Storage space = 26 * 368,640

= 9,584,640 bytes

Next, double (at least) the space that you have just calculated. This leaves room for future growth:

Storage space = 2 * 9,584,640
= 19,169,280 bytes

You now have a good idea of the size of the hard disk that you require. Keep in mind that most users fill up their hard disks within a year. Doubling your current storage requirements is only the minimum amount of space you will require—nobody ever complains of having too much disk space.

The best way to price a hard disk is by cost per byte. For example, assume that a 10-megabyte hard disk costs $300.00 while a 20-megabyte disk costs $400.00. By comparing the cost per byte, as shown here, you can better determine how much your disk storage space is costing you:

Disk Type	Actual Storage	Hypothetical Cost	Cost per Byte
10MB disk	10,653,696 bytes	$300.00	35,512.3 bytes/dollar
20MB disk	21,411,840 bytes	$400.00	53,529.6 bytes/dollar

Just as the size of a disk can vary, so too can the disk's speed. Earlier in this reference you learned about disk access time, which is the most common indicator of your disk's performance capabilities. Compare the access times of each of the disks that you are considering. You will probably find that as the access time decreases (meaning faster performance), the cost of the disk increases.

To determine if the added expense is cost-effective, you must consider how much time you will be spending at your computer each day, along with the type of applications that you will be running. If you will be spending several hours a day with your system, the faster disk-access time will quickly pay for itself. Likewise, if you are running database applications that continually access your disk (called *disk-intensive* programs), the faster disk-access time will probably again prove cost-effective. In the long run, a cheaper hard disk is not always the best buy.

Glancing through any computer magazine will demonstrate that the number of mail-order companies selling hard disk drives is overwhelming. In most cases, mail order companies provide a very good product at a very good price. The difficulty in acquiring a hard disk in this manner is its installation and repair.

Fixed disks are not easy to install. Most users, therefore, should have their computer's disk installed for them by a professional. Also, should your hard disk not work or later become damaged, you will again have to mail the disk back to the retailer. If your hard disk plays a critical role in your daily computer use, you may not want to waste the amount of time that can be consumed by mailing the disk to and from the retailer.

▶ PREPARING YOUR HARD DISK FOR USE

Depending on how much work your computer retailer has done for you, the steps that you must perform before you can use your hard disk will vary. First, if you are using a PC AT or an AT compatible and your system displays the message

162 - System Options Error - (Run SETUP)

when you turn on your computer's power, you will need to boot the Setup disk provided in the "Guide to Operations" manual that accompanied your system. When your system prompts

SELECT AN OPTION

0 - SYSTEM CHECKOUT
1 - FORMAT DISKETTE
2 - COPY DISKETTE
3 - PREPARE SYSTEM FOR MOVING
4 - SETUP
9 - END DIAGNOSTICS

SELECT THE ACTION DESIRED
?

select the SETUP option and press ENTER. You will need to know your disk type number, which is specified in the documentation that accompanies your disk or is available from your retailer. If you had your hard disk installed for you, you probably will not have to perform these steps.

To begin, place your DOS Programs disk in drive A and restart your system. When DOS displays its prompt, issue the command

A> DIR C:

In this case, "C" is the disk-drive letter that corresponds to your hard disk. If DOS displays the message

Invalid drive specification

DOS has never been told about your hard disk, so you will have to run the DOS FDISK command. If, instead, your system displays the message

General failure reading drive C
Abort, Retry, Fail?

DOS has already been told about the disk (by FDISK; someone else may have performed this step for you), but the disk has never been formatted for use by DOS.

If DOS displays a directory listing of the files on drive C, your hard disk has already been set up so that you can run DOS. To see if the system can successfully start DOS, open the disk latch on drive A and press the CTRL-ALT-DEL key combination to restart DOS. If your system starts successfully, displaying the C prompt or the DATE and TIME commands, you can proceed to the next section. If, instead, your system displays the message

Non-System disk or disk error
Replace and strike any key when ready

your disk was not correctly formatted to start DOS. Notify the person who installed DOS on your disk for you, and tell them that you plan to reformat your disk. If possible, have them assist you in the process. The correct FORMAT command will be discussed later in this section.

If DOS displayed the message

Invalid drive specification

when you issued the command

A> DIR C:

you will need to invoke the DOS FDISK command to inform DOS about your hard disk:

A> DIR FDISK

Volume in drive A is MS330PP01
Directory of A:\

FDISK   COM 48919   07-24-87 12:00a
     1 File(s) 5120 bytes free

As you can see, FDISK is an *external* DOS command. (An *external command* is a DOS command that is stored on disk, while an *internal* command is stored in memory.) Before you examine this command, let's review several key concepts and terms.

When hard disks were first released, it was not uncommon for programmers to use other operating systems in addition to DOS. To simplify their development efforts, the programmers placed both operating systems on the disk. To keep from mixing up operating system files, a programmer would logically divide the disk into fixed regions for each system. These regions, called *partitions,* look like this:

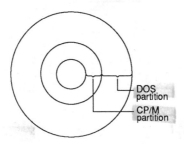

Today, most users only want to put DOS on their disks. Although it might seem that fixed-disk partitions are therefore unnecessary, this is not always the case. By default, DOS versions 3.3 and earlier only support drives of 32 megabytes. Thus, if you have purchased a 40-megabyte disk, for example, DOS only allows you to use 32 megabytes for drive C. To use the remaining disk space, you must create an extended DOS partition:

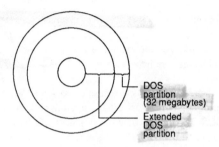

The extended partition can contain any amount of disk space. However, within this partition, you must create *logical* disk drives (drive D, drive E, and so on), each of which cannot exceed 32 megabytes:

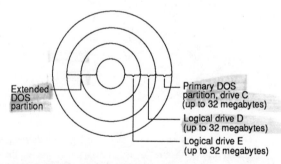

If you are using DOS version 4.0, however, your primary DOS partition can be any length, eliminating the need for you to use extended partitions.

To define your hard disk's primary and extended DOS partitions, invoke FDISK as shown here:

A> FDISK

FDISK will respond with

Fixed Disk Setup Program Version 3.30
(C)Copyright Microsoft Corp. 1987

FDISK Options

Current Fixed Disk Drive: 1

Choose one of the following:
1. Create DOS partition
2. Change Active Partition
3. Delete DOS partition
4. Display Partition Information

Enter choice: [1]

Press ESC to return to DOS

To create the primary DOS partition that you will later use to start DOS, type **1** and press ENTER. FDISK will present a new menu:

Create DOS Partition

Current Fixed Disk Drive: 1

      1. Create Primary DOS partition
      2. Create Extended DOS partition

Enter choice: [1]

Press ESC to return to FDISK Options

Again, since you are going to create a primary DOS partition, type **1** and press ENTER. FDISK will display

Create Primary DOS Partition

Current Fixed Disk Drive: 1

Do you wish to use the maximum size
for a DOS partition and make the DOS
partition active (Y/N).........? [Y]

Press ESC to return to FDISK Options

    In most cases, you will want FDISK to create a primary DOS partition that is as large as possible. Therefore, type **Y** and press ENTER. FDISK will create the partition, restart DOS, and display

System will now restart

Insert DOS diskette in drive A:
Press any key when ready...

Place your bootable DOS floppy disk in drive A and press
ENTER.

When DOS restarts, your disk is ready for formatting.
Enter the command

    A> FORMAT C: /S

The /S qualifier directs FORMAT to make your hard disk
bootable. Once this command completes, your hard disk is
ready for use by DOS. If your hard disk is 30 megabytes or
smaller, you are ready to continue on to the next section. If
you have a larger hard disk, you will need to use FDISK to
define your extended DOS partitions and additional logical
disk drives (D, E, and so on).

To create an extended DOS partition, again invoke the
FDISK command:

    A> FDISK

As before, FDISK will respond with

    Fixed Disk Setup Program Version 3.30
    (C)Copyright Microsoft Corp. 1987

    FDISK Options

    Current Fixed Disk Drive: 1

    Choose one of the following:

        1. Create DOS partition
        2. Change Active Partition

3. Delete DOS partition
4. Display Partition Information

Enter choice: [1]

Press ESC to return to DOS

Again, select option 1 and FDISK will display

Create DOS Partition

Current Hard Disk Drive: 1

1. Create Primary DOS partition
2. Create Extended DOS partition

Enter choice: [1]

Press ESC to return to FDISK Options

In this case, since you are creating an extended DOS partition, select option 2 and press ENTER. FDISK will respond with

Create Extended DOS Partition

Current Fixed Disk Drive: 1

Partition	Status	Type	Start	End	Size
C: 1	A	PRI DOS	0	523	524

Total disk space is 965 cylinders.
Maximum space available for partition
is 441 cylinders

Enter partition size...........: [441]

Press ESC to return to FDISK Options

FDISK is displaying the current number of cylinders that
it can use for an extended DOS partition. In most cases, you
will want to use this entire amount, so press ENTER. FDISK
will respond with

Create Logical DOS Drive(s)

No logical drives defined

Total partition size is 441 cylinders.

Maximum space available for logical
drive is 441 cylinders.

Enter logical drive size........: [441]

Press ESC to return to FDISK Options

FDISK has created to your extended partition. You must now create a logical disk drive (drive D):

Create Logical DOS Drive(s)

Drv Start End Size

D: 524 964 441

All available space in the Extended DOS partition is assigned to logical drives.

Logical DOS drive created, drive letters changed or added

Press ESC to return to FDISK Options

In this case, the logical disk drive (D) consumed all of the disk space in the extended partition. If you select option 4 from the menu

Fixed Disk Setup Program Version 3.30
(C)Copyright Microsoft Corp. 1987

FDISK Options

Current Fixed Disk Drive: 1

Choose one of the following:

1. Create DOS partition
2. Change Active Partition
3. Delete DOS partition
4. Display Partition Information

Enter choice: [1]

Press ESC to return to DOS

FDISK will display your current disk usage:

Display Partition Information

Current Fixed Disk Drive: 1

Partition	Status	Type	Start	End	Size
C: 1	A	PRI DOS	0	523	524
2		EXT DOS	524	964	441

Total disk space is 965 cylinders.

The Extended DOS partition contains logical DOS drives. Do you want to display logical drive information? [Y]

Press ESC to return to FDISK Options

Your logical disk drive (D) is now ready for formatting by DOS. Press the ESC key to terminate FDISK and return to DOS.

▶ ORGANIZING FILES ON YOUR DISK

Files allow you to store programs and information. Just as you create, modify, rename, and delete the files containing your papers at work, you can perform these operations with your files stored on disk. In a similar manner, just as most offices use a filing cabinet to organize files, DOS allows you to logically divide your disk into DOS subdirectories, which improve your disk organization.

Each time you issue the DOS DIR command, DOS displays a list of the files that reside on your disk:

```
A> DIR

Volume in drive A is MS330PP01
Directory of  A:\

4201      CPI      17089    07-24-87  12:00a
5202      CPI        459    07-24-87  12:00a
ANSI      SYS       1647    07-24-87  12:00a
 :         :          :        :         :
SORT      EXE       1946    07-24-87  12:00a
SUBST     EXE      10552    07-24-87  12:00a
SYS       COM       4725    07-24-87  12:00a
     34 File(s)  5120 bytes free
```

This list is called a *directory*. As you add a file to your disk, DOS places the name, the size, and date and time stamps for the file into the directory list. When you later delete the file, DOS removes the directory entry for the file.

If you have been using DOS for some time, you are probably aware of how fast your directory list can grow because of your day-to-day operations. When your directory list becomes too large, you may have difficulty locating a specific file. In addition, once your directory list becomes too long, DOS will not allow you to create additional files on the disk, regardless of the amount of available disk space.

Using a 360K floppy disk as an example, let's see how DOS restricts the number of files that a disk can store. First, a directory is nothing more than a list of files. Each time you format a disk for use by DOS, DOS places a master directory on the disk. In the case of a 360K floppy disk, DOS creates a directory large enough to store 112 files, as shown here:

FILENAME	COMMAND		SYS	
EXT	COM		COM	
ATTRIBUTE	0		0	
RESERVED	0		0	
TIME	12:00:00	• • •	12:00:00	32 bytes
DATE	06/30/88		06/30/88	
STARTING LOCATION	114		238	
SIZE	25,276		4,725	
File 1			File 112	

Once the floppy disk contains 112 files in the master directory, DOS has no room for another file, regardless of the amount of available space on the disk. If you attempt to create a 113th file, DOS will display

File creation error

Even if you are using a 10- or 20-megabyte hard disk, DOS still restricts the number of files that you can place in the master directory. The following table illustrates the number of files that DOS allows for each disk type:

Disk Space	Maximum Number of Files in the Root Directory
160K	64
180K	
320K	112
360K	
1.2MB	224
Hard disk	Based on partition size

DOS limits the number of files because it sets aside a specific number of sectors on each disk in which to store the master directory. In the case of a 360K disk, DOS sets aside seven 512- bytes sectors for this directory. If you use the equation

Directory entries = (number of sectors) * (sector size)/
32 bytes per entry

$$= 512 * 7 / 32$$

$$= 112$$

the 112-file limitation becomes clearer.

The only way you can place more files on your disk than specified in the previous table is if you use DOS subdirectories. A DOS directory contains a list of files; a DOS *subdirectory* is simply a smaller list of related files.

Before you create the DOS subdirectories on your hard disk that you will use on a regular basis, you should first experiment with subdirectories by creating and manipulating several sample directories on a newly formatted floppy disk. Since you have a floppy-disk-drive available, place a newly formatted disk in drive A and perform the following DOS subdirectory manipulation commands. First issue the DOS DIR command:

```
A> DIR

Volume in drive A has no label
Directory of  A:\

File not found

A>
```

As you can see, no files currently reside on the disk. However, the directory listing does tell you that DOS is listing the master directory:

```
Volume in drive A has no label
Directory of  A:\
```

Many computer users refer to the master directory as a disk's *root directory*. As you will soon see, the other DOS subdirectories that you will create appear to grow out from the root directory, just as branches grow from a tree.

As an example, let's use DOS subdirectories to organize files that contain your monthly bills, salary, and tax notes. To do so, you will create three DOS subdirectories:

Subdirectory	Purpose
BILLS	Stores files containing monthly bills
SALARY	Stores files containing monthly salary information
TAXNOTES	Stores files containing notes about tax-deductible expenses

Each time you create a DOS file that falls into one of these categories, you will place the file into the corresponding subdirectory. This is similar to placing a file folder in a specific drawer of a filing cabinet, as shown here:

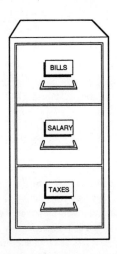

To create a DOS subdirectory, you must use the DOS MKDIR command. For example, to create the BILLS subdirectory, use the command

```
A> MKDIR \BILLS
```

The MKDIR command directs DOS to create a subdirectory called BILLS. The backslash (\) before the name directs DOS to create the subdirectory within the root directory (\). Later in this section you will learn that there are times when you need to include the backslash before a directory name, while at other times you won't. For now, however, simply include the backslash as specified.

A directory listing of the disk in drive A now reveals

```
A> DIR

Volume in drive A has no label
Directory of  A:\

BILLS    <DIR>      8-02-88  12:44p
     1 File(s)  359424 bytes free
```

Note that DOS has replaced the file-size entry of the subdirectory with "<DIR>", which informs you that BILLS is a DOS subdirectory.

To create the SALARY subdirectory, repeat the MKDIR command as

```
A> MKDIR \SALARY
```

Due to MKDIR's frequent use, DOS allows you to abbreviate the MKDIR command as MD. Create the third DOS subdirectory, TAXNOTES, as shown here:

A> MD \TAXNOTES

A directory listing of the disk now reveals

A> DIR

Volume in drive A has no label
Directory of A:\

BILLS	<DIR>	8-02-88	12:44p
SALARY	<DIR>	8-02-88	12:44p
TAXNOTES	<DIR>	8-02-88	12:44p

   3 File(s) 359424 bytes free

The directory structure as it now stands can be diagrammed as follows:

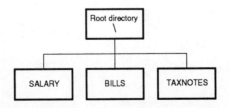

Notice how the subdirectories appear to grow from the root directory.

To create a file in a DOS subdirectory, simply precede the file name with the subdirectory name, as shown here:

```
A> COPY CON \BILLS\NOTES.DAT
This is a test file
^Z              (F6 key pressed here)
    1 File(s) copied

A>
```

A directory listing of the disk now reveals

```
A> DIR

Volume in drive A has no label
Directory of  A:\

BILLS       <DIR>      8-02-88  12:44p
SALARY      <DIR>      8-02-88  12:44p
TAXNOTES    <DIR>      8-02-88  12:44p
    3 File(s) 359424 bytes free
```

As you can see, the NOTES.DAT file does not appear in the directory listing. It should not—NOTES.DAT resides in the BILLS subdirectory. This is a directory listing of the root directory (\) only. To list the files contained in the BILLS subdirectory, simply change your DIR command to

```
A> DIR \BILLS
```

In this case, the directory listing displays the NOTES.DAT
file along with two other directories:

```
A> DIR \BILLS

Volume in drive A has no label
Directory of  A:\BILLS

    .      <DIR>           8-02-88  12:44p
    ..     <DIR>           8-02-88  12:44p
NOTES  DAT     21      8-02-88  12:46p
      3 File(s) 358400 bytes free
```

Later in this section you will learn about the . and .. entries in
detail. For now, just note that DOS places these two entries
in every subdirectory that it creates.

If you use DIR to display the contents of a file in the directory, as in

```
A> DIR \SALARY
```

DOS will display

```
A> DIR \SALARY

Volume in drive A has no label
Directory of  A:\SALARY

    .      <DIR>        8-02-88  12:44p
    ..     <DIR>        8-02-88  12:44p
      2 File(s) 358400 bytes free
```

Although the SALARY subdirectory does not yet contain any
files, DOS still displays the . and .. subdirectories, which it
places in every subdirectory.

To display the contents of the NOTES.DAT file, precede
the file name with the subdirectory name, as shown here:

```
A> TYPE \BILLS\NOTES.DAT
This is a test file

A>
```

As you can see, when you work with DOS subdirectories, the
DOS file-manipulation commands do not change. Instead,
you simply precede the names of the files to be manipulated
with the corresponding subdirectory name. For example, to
copy the NOTES.DAT file from the BILLS subdirectory to
the TAXNOTES subdirectory, simply issue the command

```
A> COPY \BILLS\NOTES.DAT \TAXNOTES\NOTES.DAT
    1 File(s) copied
```

Likewise, to copy the same file to the SALARY subdirectory
by using DOS wildcard characters, enter

```
A> COPY \BILLS\NOTES.DAT \TAXNOTES\*.*
```

Just as DOS defines the current or default disk as the drive
that it searches for DOS commands or files (unless your command line specifies otherwise), DOS also defines the *current*
directory. As you saw in the previous directory listings, unless you told DOS to list the contents of a specific subdirectory, DOS listed the files in the root directory:

```
A> DIR
```

```
Volume in drive A has no label
Directory of  A:\

BILLS        <DIR>      8-02-88  12:44p
SALARY       <DIR>      8-02-88  12:44p
TAXNOTES     <DIR>      8-02-88  12:44p
      3 File(s) 359424 bytes free
```

This is because the root directory was your current, or default, directory. However, DOS also allows you to change the current directory by means of the DOS CHDIR command. To select the BILLS subdirectory as your current directory, for example, use the command

```
A> CHDIR \BILLS
```

A directory listing of drive A now reveals

```
A> DIR
```

```
Volume in drive A has no label
Directory of  A:\BILLS

.         <DIR>      8-02-88  12:44p
..        <DIR>      8-02-88  12:44p
NOTES  DAT  21    8-02-88  12:46p
      3 File(s) 357376 bytes free
```

As you can see, DOS displayed the contents of the BILLS subdirectory. If you create a second file in this directory, as

```
A> COPY CON MESSAGE.TXT
This is also a sample file.
^Z
       1 File(s) copied

A>
```

DOS will create the file in the BILLS directory, as shown in this directory listing:

```
A> DIR

Volume in drive A has no label
Directory of  A:\BILLS

   .            <DIR>        8-02-88   12:44p
   ..           <DIR>        8-02-88   12:44p
NOTES     DAT 21      8-02-88   12:46p
MESSAGE TXT 29       8-02-88   12:48p
       4 File(s) 356352 bytes free
```

BILLS is your current directory for drive A. If you simply type **CHDIR** without specifying a directory name, DOS will display the current directory name, as shown here:

```
A> CHDIR
A:\BILLS

A>
```

To select the root directory once again as your current directory, simply issue the command

```
A> CHDIR \
```

A directory listing of your disk reveals that the root directory is now your current directory:

```
A> DIR

Volume in drive A has no label
Directory of  A:\

BILLS        <DIR>      8-02-88   12:44p
SALARY       <DIR>      8-02-88   12:44p
TAXNOTES     <DIR>      8-02-88   12:44p
        3 File(s) 359424 bytes free
```

DOS allows you to abbreviate the CHDIR command as CD. Using this abbreviation, select the SALARY subdirectory as your current directory:

```
A> CD \SALARY
```

Creating DOS subdirectories within your root directory increases your file organization; dividing a subdirectory into additional directories increases that organization as well. For example, you might want to track your salary files by month, as shown here:

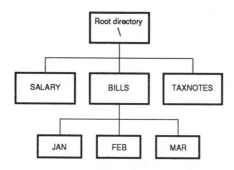

To do so, you need to create the additional subdirectories:

```
A> MKDIR \SALARY\JAN
A> MKDIR \SALARY\FEB
A> MKDIR \SALARY\MAR
```

A directory listing of the SALARY subdirectory now reveals

```
A> DIR \SALARY

Volume in drive A has no label
Directory of  A:\SALARY

.         <DIR>      8-02-88  12:44p
..        <DIR>      8-02-88  12:44p
JAN       <DIR>      8-02-88  12:51p
FEB       <DIR>      8-02-88  12:51p
MAR       <DIR>      8-02-88  12:51p
      5 File(s) 353280 bytes free
```

If you select the \SALARY\JAN subdirectory as your current directory by entering

[C:\] CHDIR \SALARY\JAN

a directory listing of the subdirectory reveals

A> DIR

Volume in drive A has no label
Directory of A:\SALARY\JAN

```
.       <DIR>       8-02-88  12:51p
..      <DIR>       8-02-88  12:51p
        2 File(s) 353280 bytes free
```

As you can see, DOS has created the . and .. subdirectories as previously discussed. These two subdirectories are abbreviations:

.   The current directory
..   The directory that resides immediately above the current directory

If the current directory is \SALARY, . abbreviates SALARY and .. references the root directory. Likewise, if the current directory is \SALARY\JAN, . abbreviates \SALARY\JAN and .. references \SALARY. If you perform a directory listing of the . directory, DOS will display a directory listing of the current directory like this:

A> DIR .

Volume in drive A has no label
Directory of A:\SALARY\JAN

```
  .      <DIR>      8-02-88  12:51p
  ..     <DIR>      8-02-88  12:51p
      2 File(s) 353280 bytes free
```

Likewise, if you perform the directory listing .., DOS will display the contents of the directory that resides immediately
above the current directory:

A> DIR ..

Volume in drive A has no label
Directory of A:\SALARY

```
  .       <DIR>      8-02-88  12:44p
  ..      <DIR>      8-02-88  12:44p
  JAN     <DIR>      8-02-88  12:51p
  FEB     <DIR>      8-02-88  12:51p
  MAR     <DIR>      8-02-88  12:51p
       5 File(s) 353280 bytes free
```

   Most users do not use these abbreviations on a regular
basis. However, because DOS creates them in every subdirectory, you should know that they exist and what they mean.
   Just as the DOS DEL command allows you to erase a file
from disk when the file is no longer required, the DOS
RMDIR command allows you to remove a subdirectory from

a disk when you no longer need it. Using RMDIR, remove the FEB subdirectory from the SALARY subdirectory, as shown here:

A> RMDIR \SALARY\FEB

A directory listing of SALARY now reveals

A> DIR \SALARY

Volume in drive A has no label
Directory of A:\SALARY

```
.     <DIR>            8-02-88   12:44p
..    <DIR>            8-02-88   12:44p
JAN   <DIR>            8-02-88   12:51p
MAR   <DIR>            8-02-88   12:51p
      4 File(s) 354304 bytes free
```

Like MKDIR and CHDIR, the RMDIR commmand can be abbreviated. In this case, you simply use RD:

A> RD \SALARY\JAN

DOS does not allow you to remove a directory that contains files. For example, if you attempt to remove the BILLS subdirectory, which contains

A> DIR \BILLS

Volume in drive A has no label
Directory of A:\BILLS

.	<DIR>		8-02-88	12:44p
..	<DIR>		8-02-88	12:44p
NOTES	DAT	21	8-02-88	12:46p
MESSAGE	TXT	29	8-02-88	12:48p

4 File(s) 354304 bytes free

the RMDIR command will fail and DOS will display

Invalid path, not directory,
or directory not empty

Before you can remove a directory, you must first delete
the files that the directory contains. Also, if you attempt to
remove the current directory, the RMDIR command will fail
and DOS will display the message

Invalid path, not directory,
or directory not empty

You are now ready to proceed onward to more difficult
DOS directory manipulation commands.

► TRACKING CURRENT DIRECTORIES WITH THE PROMPT

By default, the DOS prompt contains the current disk-drive
letter followed immediately by a greater-than symbol:

A>

When you begin creating DOS subdirectories on your disk,
you should set your DOS prompt to

[$p]

by means of the DOS PROMT command, as shown here:

```
A> PROMT[$P]
[A:\]
```

When you later change subdirectories, DOS will update your prompt as shown here:

```
[A:\] CHDIR \SALARY
[A:\SALARY] CHDIR \SALARY\JAN
[A:\SALARY\JAN] CHDIR \
[A:\] B:
[B:\]
```

This allows you to quickly determine the current directory simply by examining your DOS prompt.

► THE BACKSLASH IN SUBDIRECORY NAMES

As you saw earlier, in some cases you will need to precede your directory names with a backslash, while at other times you will not. Knowing when to include the backslash depends on knowing the current directory. When a subdirectory that you want to reference resides below the current directory, you can simply specify the subdirectory name, excluding the backslash. For example, given the directory structure

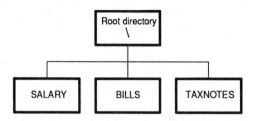

if the root directory is your current directory, you can select the SALARY subdirectory without specifying the backslash, like this:

    [A:\] CHDIR SALARY
    [A:\SALARY]

DOS allows you to perform this operation because the SALARY subdirectory resides immediately below the current directory.

Now assume that SALARY is the current directory. The command

    [A:\SALARY] CHDIR BILLS

will fail, and DOS will display

    Invalid directory

In this case, the BILLS subdirectory does not reside below the current directory, SALARY; rather, it resides below the root directory. Therefore, you must specify the backslash:

[A:\SALARY] CHDIR \BILLS
[A:\BILLS]

If you now create the TEST subdirectory with

[A:\BILLS] MKDIR TEST

DOS will create the subdirectory within the current directory, which in this case is BILLS:

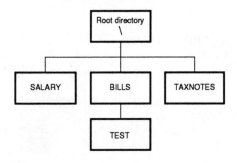

Had you instead preceded the subdirectory name with a backslash, as in

[A:\BILLS] MKDIR \TEST

DOS would have created the subdirectory in the root directory, yielding the subdirectory structure

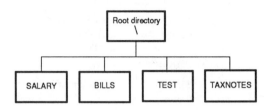

When you perform DOS subdirectory manipulation commands, ask yourself the question "Where does the subdirectory reside?" If the subdirectory resides in the current directory, you can omit the backslash. If the subdirectory resides elsewhere, you must include a complete directory name, beginning with the backslash.

▶ RULES FOR CREATING DOS SUBDIRECTORIES

As you create your DOS subdirectories, keep the following rules in mind:

- DOS subdirectory names must conform to DOS file-name standards. Each subdirectory name can contain from one to eight characters, with an optional three-character extension. For example, IBM and IBM.PC are valid DOS subdirectory names.

- If you do not start your subdirectory name in the root directory by placing a backslash at the front of the name, DOS will create the subdirectory in the current directory.

- If you want to create a DOS subdirectory on a disk drive other than the current default, simply include a disk-drive specifier in your MKDIR command line, as in MKDIR B:\TESTDIR.

- DOS will not allow you to create a subdirectory name that is the same as the name of a file that currently resides in the same directory.

- Do not create a subdirectory called \DEV. DOS uses a hidden internal subdirectory called DEV to perform device I/O operations. To copy a file to your printer, for example, you can use the command

    A> COPY FILENAME.EXT \DEV\PRN

- DOS allows you to create a unlimited number of files and subdirectories in directories other than the root. However, the root directory only supports a limited number of files.

▶ WHAT IS A PATH NAME?

Many of the DOS commands require you to specify a complete *path name* for your DOS files. Simply stated, a path name is a list of the subdirectories that DOS must traverse in order to locate your files or programs. Earlier, you issued the command

    A> TYPE \BILLS\NOTES.DAT

Since the NOTES.DAT file resides in a DOS subdirectory, you not only have to specify the name of the file to be displayed, but also the name of the subdirectory in which the file resides. Given the command

A> TYPE \SALARY\JAN\01-07-89.PAY

the file name is 01-07-89.PAY, while the subdirectories in the path are \SALARY\JAN. Put together, the subdirectories and file name produce a complete DOS path name. If a DOS command directs you to specify a path name, it is simply asking you to include not only the file name, but also the subdirectory in which the file resides. Keep in mind that DOS path names cannot exceed 63 characters.

► PUTTING DOS COMMANDS ON YOUR HARD DISK

If someone else has installed DOS on your hard disk for you, you may at this point have to move some files around on your disk before it is optimally configured. If, instead, you have just finished formatting your hard disk as discussed at the beginning of this reference, simply select drive C as your default drive:

[A:\] C:
[C:\]

Next, create the DOS subdirectory, as shown here:

[C:\] MKDIR \DOS

With your DOS Programs disk in drive A, copy all of the files from the disk into the DOS subdirectory:

    [C:\] COPY A:*.* \DOS

When this command completes, place your DOS Supplemental Programs disk in drive A and repeat the COPY command, copying all of the files that the disk contains to the DOS sub-directory:

    [C:\] COPY A:*.* \DOS

Next, make sure that the COMMAND.COM file resides in the root directory:

    [C:\] DIR \COMMAND.COM

    Volume in drive C has no label
    Directory of C:\

    File not found

    [C:\]

If it does not, copy the file from your DOS Programs disk:

    [C:\] COPY A:\COMMAND.COM \COMMAND.COM

Place your DOS disks in a safe location. You can now proceed to the next section.

If someone else has placed DOS on your hard disk for you, you will still want to create a directory called DOS in which to store your DOS commands. Before doing so, verify that this subdirectory does not already exist on your disk:

[C:\] DIR \DOS

Volume in drive C has no label
Directory of C:\

File not found

[C:\]

If the directory does not exist, create it by using MKDIR:

[C:\] MKDIR \DOS

If you have your original DOS disks, issue the COPY commands shown previously in this section, copying the files from your DOS Programs disk and Supplemental Programs disk to the DOS subdirectory:

[C:\] COPY A:*.* \DOS

Next, you must examine the files that reside in your disk's root directory. To do so, issue the command

[C:\] DIR \

If you have a printer available, you may want to redirect the output of the command to a printer, giving you a printed listing of the files:

    [C:\] DIR \ > PRN

Your goal is to either delete the files that reside in your root directory or move them into DOS subdirectories. When you are through, your root directory should, at most, contain only the files

COMMAND.COM
CONFIG.SYS
AUTOEXEC.BAT

The remainder of the root directory entries should be sub-directories such as DOS. If the CONFIG.SYS and AUTO-EXEC.BAT files are not on your disk, don't worry; you will create them later in this reference.

In most cases, if your root directory is full of files, most of them are probably DOS commands that you can delete. To help you determine which files you can delete, obtain a printed listing of your DOS subdirectory, as shown here:

    [C:\] DIR \DOS > PRN

With this listing in hand, you can identify several files that you can remove from the root directory.

At first, it may appear that moving all of the files from the root directory into your DOS subdirectories is a considerable chore. However, doing this is the first step toward organizing your hard disk, which in turn leads to improved performance. Once you have your root directory cleaned up, you should not have to perform this task again.

► ## EXECUTING EXTERNAL COMMANDS IN SUBDIRECTORIES

Earlier, you learned that to manipulate files residing in DOS subdirectories, you have to specify a complete DOS path name for the file as in

    [A:\] TYPE \BILLS\NOTES

In a similar manner, to execute DOS external commands that reside in a subdirectory, you need to precede the command name with the name of the subdirectory in which the command resides. In the case of your DOS commands, you simply need to specify the DOS subdirectory as shown here:

    [C:\] \DOS\LABEL

In this case, DOS will locate the LABEL command within the DOS subdirectory and respond with

    Volume in drive C has no label

    Volume label (11 characters, ENTER for none)?

To cancel the command, simply use the CTRL-BREAK key combination. (The BREAK key is the same as the PAUSE key.) You could have also selected the DOS subdirectory as the current default with

    [C:\] CHDIR DOS
    [C:\DOS]

and have then issued the command as

[C:\DOS] LABEL

However, because DOS allows you to perform the same function in one command, there is no reason to use two.

If drive C is not your current disk drive, you can still invoke the DOS commands that reside on drive C by specifying the disk- drive letter, followed by a complete path name to the command, as shown here:

[A:\] C:\DOS\DISKCOPY A: B:

All of the external DOS commands that reside in the subdirectory DOS can be invoked in this manner.

► INSTALLING OTHER PROGRAMS ON YOUR DISK

Now that you have DOS readily available on your hard disk, you are ready to install other applications, such as your word processor or spreadsheet. Keep in mind that each program should be placed in its own subdirectory. In most cases, the documentation that accompanied your software will recommend a subdirectory name that you should use. If not, decide on a meaningful name, and use MKDIR to create the subdirectory:

[C:\] MKDIR \WORDPROC

Next, copy all of the files from the floppy disk to the specified subdirectory:

[C:\] COPY A:*.* \WORDPROC*.*

In most cases, you will simply select the subdirectory containing the application program as the current directory when you want to run the application program:

[C:\] CHDIR \WORDPROC

Most word processors and spreadsheets fully support DOS subdirectories. Therefore, you might want to create additional subdirectories in which to store data below the directories that contain your programs. In the case of a word processor, for example, you might consider creating subdirectories to store letters, reports, and memos.

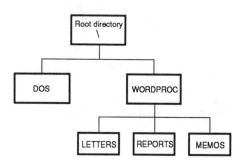

Remember, DOS subdirectories exist to help you organize your files; if you don't use them, they can't help you. Also keep in mind your original goal of restricting the root directory to the COMMAND.COM, CONFIG.SYS, and AUTO-EXEC.BAT files.

Eventually, your directory structure may become quite complex, as shown here:

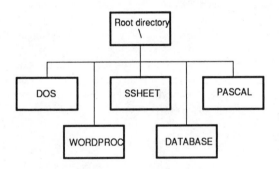

▶ GIVING YOUR DISK A NAME

Each time you issue a DIR command, DOS displays the name of the disk that it is examining:

    A> DIR

    Volume in drive A is MS330PP01◄── Disk name
    Directory of A:\

If the disk does not have a name, DOS displays

```
Volume in drive C has no label
Directory of  C:\
```

The DOS LABEL command allows you to assign a *volume label* (or name) to your hard disk. The easiest way to invoke LABEL is simply as

```
[C:\] \DOS\LABEL
```

When DOS locates the LABEL.COM file in the DOS sub-directory, it will execute the LABEL command, which in turn displays

```
[C:\] \DOS\LABEL
```

```
Volume in drive C has no label
```

```
Volume label (11 characters, ENTER for none)?
```

DOS label names can contain up to 11 characters. All of the characters that are valid for DOS file names are valid for label names as well. In addition, DOS allows you to use the space character in your label names. For a hard disk, most users assign a name like "DOS 3-3":

```
[C:\] \DOS\LABEL
```

```
Volume in drive C has no label
```

```
Volume label (11 characters, ENTER for none)? DOS 3-3
```

When you later perform a directory listing of the disk, DOS will display the label name:

[C:\] DIR

Volume in drive C is DOS 3-3
Directory of C:\

If you mistype a volume label or use an invalid character,
LABEL will simply prompt you to enter a new label name:

Volume in drive C is DOS 3-3

Volume label (11 characters, ENTER for none)? DOS 3.3

Invalid characters in volume label
Volume label (11 characters, ENTER for none)?

LABEL also allows you to include the desired label name
in the command line, as shown here:

[C:\]\DOS\LABEL DOSDISK

To change your disk label name, simply invoke LABEL and
type in a new name, as shown here:

Volume in drive C is DOSDISK

Volume label (11 characters, ENTER for none)? DOS 3-3

If you later decide that you want to delete an existing name,
press ENTER at the label-name prompt. LABEL will then ask
you whether or not you want to delete the disk name:

Delete current volume label (Y/N)?

To delete the name, type **Y** and press ENTER; to leave the name unchanged, type **N** and press ENTER.

Disk label names are very helpful in organizing your floppy disks when several disks are used in the same application. If each disk has a unique label name assigned to it, software programs can examine the floppy disk, ensuring that you have the correct disk in the drive. Hard-disk users should assign a label name to the disk that contains the current DOS version number (assuming the disk does not have a specific function). As you will see later, the DOS CHKDSK command not only displays the volume name, but also the date on which the volume name was assigned to the disk. By examining this date, you can determine when this version of DOS was installed on the disk.

Once you assign a disk volume name to a disk, the DOS VOL command allows you to display the volume name, as shown here:

```
[C:\] VOL
```

```
Volume in drive C is DOS 3-3
```

Since VOL is an internal DOS command that resides in your computer's memory, you do not have to specify a subdirectory name before the command. The only time you need to include a subdirectory path is when the command is an external command that resides on disk.

► PROTECTING YOUR FILES

One of the first things that you should always do with your original floppy and microfloppy disks is to write-protect them. In the case of the floppy disk, this is accomplished by covering the write-protect notch, as shown here:

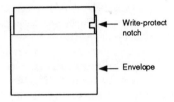

Thus, you protect your original files against errant DOS commands such as

A> DEL *.*

If you are using a hard disk, however, you cannot write-protect your disk in this way—you have to use another method of protecting your files. The DOS ATTRIB command provides one solution. If you perform the DIR command

[C:\] DIR \DOS\ATTRIB

you will find that ATTRIB is an external DOS command:

[C:\] DIR \DOS\ATTRIB

Volume in drive C is DOS 3-3
Directory of C:\DOS

```
ATTRIB    EXE    10656   7-24-87 12:00a
    1 File(s) 30730240 bytes free
```

Each of the files that DOS creates has a set of characteristics, called *attributes,* which define the ways that DOS can manipulate them. One of these attributes is called a *read-only* attribute. When you set a file to read-only, you tell DOS that it can type, print, execute, or copy the contents of the file, but not change or delete it. This is an ideal attribute for DOS commands, which you will never modify. By setting your DOS commands to read-only, you will not be able to delete or overwrite them accidentally, providing a level of protection against errant DOS commands.

To set your DOS files to read-only, issue the command

```
[C:\] \DOS\ATTRIB +R \DOS\*.*
```

ATTRIB, in this case, will set all of the files that reside in the subdirectory DOS to read-only.

To better understand how ATTRIB protects your files, create the following file:

```
[C:\] COPY CON TEST.DAT
This is an ATTRIB test file
^Z
        1 File(s) copied

[C:\]
```

Next, set the file to read-only:

```
[C:\] \DOS\ATTRIB +R TEST.DAT
```

Once you have done so, issue the following DEL command:

    [C:\] DEL TEST.DAT

Since you have marked the file as read-only, DOS cannot delete the file. DEL will fail and display the message

    Access Denied

If you try to overwrite the file by using COPY, as in

    [C:\] COPY COMMAND.COM TEST.DAT

the command will fail and DOS will display

    File creation error

DOS does allow you to type, print, execute, or copy a read-only file, as shown here:

    [C:\] TYPE TEST.DAT
    This is an ATTRIB test file

    [C:\]

If you later decide that you really want to delete the TEST.DAT file, ATTRIB allows you to remove the read-only attribute in this manner:

    [C:\] \DOS\ATTRIB -R TEST.DAT

Once you do so, the file is no longer protected, and a command such as

[C:\] DEL TEST.DAT

succeeds. Later in this reference you will use other features of the ATTRIB command when you copy files from your hard disk to floppies.

► DEFINING A COMMAND-FILE SEARCH PATH

Each time you execute a DOS command, DOS first checks to see if the command is an internal command that resides in your computer's memory. If it is not, DOS then checks to see if the command is an EXE, COM, or a BAT file that resides on disk. As you have learned, to execute commands that reside in DOS subdirectories, you simply precede the command name with the specific subdirectory that contains the command

[C:\] \DOS\LABEL

DOS, however, provides a means of simplifying the execution of your external commands: the PATH command. PATH is an internal command that allows you to define a set of directories in which DOS will search for your external commands when it fails to locate the command in the current directory or the subdirectory specified in the command line.

For example, since your DOS commands reside in the DOS subdirectory on drive C, you should issue the command

[C:\] PATH C:\DOS

Once you do so, you can simply issue your DOS commands as follows:

[C:\] LABEL

regardless of what the current directory is. When DOS fails to find LABEL as an internal command or in the current directory, it checks to see if you have defined a command-file search path with the DOS PATH command. If you have, DOS examines each of the entries contained in the path to see if the command exists in one of the specified subdirectories. In this case, DOS will search the DOS subdirectory on drive C and locate the command.

If DOS still fails to locate the command after searching the specified subdirectories in the command-file search path, it will display the message

Bad command or file name

DOS also allows you to specify multiple subdirectories in your PATH command. DOS will examine these in the specified order as it searches for external commands. For example, given the command

[C:\] PATH C:\DOS;C:\UTIL;C:\WORDPROC

if DOS fails to locate a command as specified in the command line, it will first see if the command exists in the DOS subdirectory. If it does, DOS will execute the command. If it does not, DOS will continue the search in the UTIL subdirectory, followed by WORDPROC. Notice that semicolons separate each of the different subdirectories that DOS is to search.

Since DOS always searches the directories in the order in which they are specified in the PATH command, always place the subdirectories most likely to contain your command files first in the command-file search path. DOS will then find your files sooner, saving you time.

To display the current command-file search path, simply invoke the PATH command without specifying command-line arguments:

```
[C:\] PATH
PATH=C:\DOS;C:\UTIL;C:\WORDPROC

[C:\]
```

Likewise, to delete your command-file search path, place a semicolon in your PATH command line as shown here:

```
[C:\] PATH ;
```

Once you delete your command-file search path in this manner, DOS will again only search for commands as internal commands in memory, or as external commands in the current directory or the specified directory in the command line. As you will see, most users place the desired command path in the AUTOEXEC.BAT file, which will be discussed later in this reference.

▶ DEFINING A SEARCH PATH FOR DATA FILES

DOS version 3.3 provides the APPEND command, which allows you to define a list of subdirectories that DOS will examine in search of your data files. Assume, for example, that your hard disk contains the subdirectories SALARY, BILLS, and TAXNOTES. Select the root as your current directory:

    A> CD \

The command

    A> TYPE NOTES.DAT
    File not found

    A>

fails because DOS cannot find the NOTES.DAT file in the current directory. However, if you include BILLS in the data-file search path, as in

    A> APPEND A:\BILLS

the TYPE command results in

    A> TYPE NOTES.DAT
    This is a test file

    A>

The command succeeds because DOS now searches each directory in the data-file search path. To include all three of the BILLS, SALARY, and TAXNOTES directories, your APPEND command would become

    A> APPEND A:\BILLS;A:\SALARY;A:\TAXNOTES

Just as with the PATH command, if you simply type **AP-PEND** and press ENTER, DOS will display your current data-file search path:

```
A> APPEND
APPEND=A:\BILLS;A:\SALARY;A:\TAXNOTES

A>
```

Likewise, to delete this search path, simply type **APPEND** followed immediately by a semicolon:

```
[C:\] APPEND ;
```

By default, not all DOS commands recognize the data-file search path. Thus, if you want to expand the number of applications that use the data-file search path, the first time you invoke APPEND you must use the /X qualifier, as shown here:

```
A> APPEND /X
```

Also by default, APPEND does not place an entry in your DOS environment:

```
[C:\] SET
COMSPEC=A:\COMMAND.COM
PATH=C:\DOS;C:\UTIL;C:\WORDPROC
PROMPT=[$p]

[C:\]
```

To have it do so (although this is not required for the command to work), use the /E qualifier the first time that you invoke APPEND:

A> APPEND /E

Some people are concerned that if they create a data-file search path, DOS might inadvertently delete a file, given a command such as

A> DEL FILENAME.EXT

DOS, however, has already taken this into account. If you attempt to delete a file that does not reside in the current directory or the specified directory, and DOS locates that file in the data-file search path, DOS will display the message

Access Denied

instead of deleting the file. Your files are indeed protected from errant commands.

If you have a subdirectory of data files that you use on a regular basis, you may want to include the subdirectory in a data-file search path. Remember, however, that if you place too many directories in this path, DOS will spend more time searching through files than performing useful tasks.

▶ ABBREVIATING LONG DIRECTORY NAMES

If you are using DOS subdirectories to their fullest extent, it may not take much time before your DOS path names become quite long. If you repeatedly have to access these directories, as in

```
[C:\] CHDIR \WORDPROC\LETTERS\BUSINESS
```

or

```
[C:\] TYPE \REPORTS\SALES\JULY\SOFTWARE.$$$
```

you can spend a considerable amount of time simply typing DOS subdirectory names. The DOS SUBST command allows you to abbreviate long, commonly used subdirectory names with a simple disk-drive letter (D:, E:, F:, and so on).

To better understand how SUBST works, create the following subdirectories:

```
[C:\] MKDIR \TESTDIR
[C:\] MKDIR \TESTDIR\NEXTDIR
```

Next, create the following file:

```
[C:\] COPY CON \TESTDIR\NEXTDIR\SUBST.TXT
^Z
1 File(s copied

[C:\]
```

The DOS SUBST command allows you to abbreviate long directory names.

SUBST is an external DOS command, as you can see:

```
[C:\] DIR  SUBST

Volume in drive C is DOS 3-3
Directory of  C:\DOS

SUBST      EXE      10552   7-24-87 12:00a
      1 File(s) 30717952 bytes free
```

To abbreviate the subdirectory \TESTDIR\NEXTDIR as
drive E, issue the command

```
[C:\] SUBST E: \TESTDIR\NEXTDIR
```

If you issue a directory listing of drive E with

```
[C:\] DIR E:
```

DOS will recognize the substitution and display the contents
of the subdirectory \TESTDIR\NEXTDIR:

```
[C:\] DIR E:

Volume in drive E is DOS 3-3
Volume Serial Number is 305A-17C4
Directory of  E:\

.        <DIR>           08-02-88   5:05p
..       <DIR>           08-02-88   5:05p
SUBST   TXT      71      08-02-88   5:05p
      3 File(s) 30267392 bytes free
```

To display the contents of the SUBST.TXT file, you can use the command

```
[C:\] TYPE  E:SUBST.TXT
The DOS SUBST command allows you
to abbreviate long directory names.

[C:\]
```

To display your current directory substitutions, simply type **SUBST** with no command-line arguments:

```
[C:\] SUBST
```

In this case, DOS will display

```
[C:\] SUBST
E: => C:\TESTDIR\NEXTDIR
```

If the subdirectory that you are abbreviating contains additional DOS subdirectories, you can reference them as if they were subdirectories within drive E:

```
[C:\] CHDIR  E:\SUBDIR
```

When you later want to remove a directory substitution, use the /D qualifier in the SUBST command line, as shown here:

```
[C:\] SUBST  E: /D
```

Once you do so, if you again attempt to access drive E, DOS will display

Invalid drive specification

This makes sense, because drive E is no longer substituted.

When you use SUBST to abbreviate a directory name with a disk-drive letter, you are actually creating a logical disk drive. By default, DOS only allows you to reference drives A through E. If you are performing many directory substitutions, you will need to specify the LASTDRIVE= entry in CONFIG.SYS. This entry, for example, allows you to reference drives A through J, as shown here:

    LASTDRIVE=J

Remember, once you modify CONFIG.SYS, you must restart DOS in order for the change to take effect. Don't forget to remove the TESTDIR and NEXTDIR subdirectories from your disk before proceeding.

▶ COPYING FILES FROM YOUR HARD DISK TO FLOPPIES

Earlier, you copied files from your DOS disks to your hard disk the command

    [C:\] COPY A:*.* C:\DOS*.*

Since your hard disk had much more available disk space than the files on the floppy disks required, the COPY command succeeded. However, if you reverse this process and copy files from your DOS subdirectory back to a 360K floppy disk, the floppy disk will eventually be filled and DOS will display the error message

Insufficient disk space

Unfortunately, when you use COPY, you do not have a means of continuing the copying operation with a new floppy disk at the last file successfully copied. However, if you use the DOS XCOPY command in conjunction with the AT-TRIB command, copying files from your hard disk to floppy disk in this manner is quite straightforward.

Your file's attributes (discussed earlier in this reference) can influence how DOS manipulates the file. You have already seen the use of the read-only attribute to protect your files. In addition to the read-only attribute, DOS uses an *archive* or "backup required" attribute. Later in this reference, you will examine the DOS BACKUP command, which allows you to make duplicate copies of your hard disk files on floppy disks. If you accidentally delete a file or your hard disk becomes damaged, you will then have a backup copy of your files on floppy disk. As you will learn, one of the BACKUP command's abilities is that it can back up only the files that you have created or modified since your last BACKUP command. This makes your backup operations very fast and efficient, because BACKUP only has to back up a few files each day. BACKUP provides this capability by examining each file's archive attribute.

As it turns out, each time you modify or create a file, DOS marks the file as requiring a backup; it sets the file's archive attribute. When BACKUP later backs up the file to floppy disk, BACKUP clears the archive attribute. If you execute the DOS ATTRIB command as

[C:\] ATTRIB \DOS*.*

ATTRIB will display each file's attribute settings in the following manner:

```
[C:\] ATTRIB \DOS\*.*
A   C:\DOS\4201.CPI
A   C:\DOS\5202.CPI
A   C:\DOS\ANSI.SYS

 .    .
 .    .
 .    .

A   C:\DOS\TREE.COM
A   C:\DOS\XCOPY.EXE
A   C:\DOS\FC.EXE
```

Note the uppercase letter "A" that appears next to the file names. This letter tells you that the file's archive attribute is set; in other words, the file has been created or modified since the last BACKUP command. The uppercase letter "R" tells you that the file has been set to read-only.

By using the ATTRIB command in conjunction with the DOS XCOPY command, you can easily copy files from your hard disk to multiple floppy disks. First, set the archive attribute for all of the files in the directory that you want to copy:

```
[C:\] ATTRIB +A \DOS\*.*
```

Next, with a formatted disk in drive A, issue the command

```
[C:\] XCOPY \DOS\*.* A: /M
```

The DOS XCOPY command begins to copy the files from your DOS subdirectory. The /M qualifier directs XCOPY to copy only those files whose archive attribute is set. Since you have just set the archive attribute for all of the files in the directory, XCOPY will copy all of the files.

Each time XCOPY successfully copies a file from your hard disk to the floppy disk in drive A, the /M qualifier also directs XCOPY to clear the file's archive attribute. When the floppy disk in drive A fills and DOS displays the message

Insufficient disk space

simply insert another formatted disk in drive A and repeat the XCOPY command

[C:\] XCOPY \DOS*.* A: /M

Since XCOPY is marking each file it successfully copies by clearing the archive attribute, XCOPY has a placeholder to tell it where to continue the file-copying operation. XCOPY will start copying files to the floppy disk right where it left off.

If the subdirectory that you are copying contains additional subdirectories, the /S qualifier directs both ATTRIB and XCOPY to manipulate files that reside in subdirectories below the specified directory. To display the attributes of all of the files on your disk, use the command

[C:\] ATTRIB C:*.* /S

DISPLAYING YOUR DIRECTORY'S TREE STRUCTURE

As the complexity of your DOS subdirectories increases on your hard disk, you may eventually have difficulty remembering all of the subdirectories that you have placed on your disk, not to mention the files that the subdirectories contain. The DOS TREE command displays the directory structure of your disk, and can also display the files that each subdirectory contains. If, for example, you directory structure is

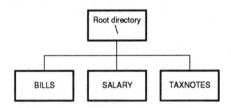

the command

    [C:\] TREE

will display

    DIRECTORY PATH LISTING

    Path: \BILLS

Sub-directories: None

Path: \SALARY

Sub-directories: None

Path: \TAXNOTES

Sub-directories: None

To display all of the files in each subdirectory as well, use the /F qualifier as shown here:

[C:\] TREE /F

▶ MAKING DOS SEE ONE DISK DRIVE AS ANOTHER

Some older software packages always look to drive A for specific files. Thus, it first seems that you must always place the disk containing these files into drive A when you execute the program. By doing this, however, you lose the advantages that your hard disk provides, since you are now apparently forced to use a floppy disk.

As a solution to this problem, DOS provides the ASSIGN command, which allows you to trick DOS into looking on one disk drive for the files that normally reside on another. For example, if you issue the command

[C:\] ASSIGN A=C

DOS will route all disk-drive references destined for drive A to drive C. If, for example, you issue the command

[C:\] DIR A:

DOS will actually display the files that reside on drive C. If you have a program that continually looks on drive A for files, and you want those files on your hard disk instead, use AS-SIGN to make DOS find the files on drive C.

Once you finish running the application that is dependent on drive A, you can restore normal disk-drive operations by simply issuing the ASSIGN command without command-line parameters:

[C:\] ASSIGN

Most users will not need the ASSIGN command. However, if you have a unique application that always looks for files on a specific disk, ASSIGN may provide you with an alternative.

▶ DISPLAYING DISK STATUS INFORMATION

Probably the best way to determine the actual usage of your hard disk is with the DOS CHKDSK command:

[C:\] DIR \DOS\CHKDSK

Volume in drive C is DOS 3-3

Directory of C:\DOS

CHKDSK   COM   9819 7-24-87 12:00a
     1 File(s) 30334976 bytes free

CHKDSK examines the disk drive that you specify in the command line and displays the following information:

- The disk volume label and the date that the volume label was assigned

- The number of bytes of data that the disk can store

- The number of hidden files on your disk, and the amount of disk space (in bytes) that these files consume

- The number of directories and subdirectories on your disk

- The amount of space consumed by user files on the disk (in bytes)

- The number of bytes available for storing information on the disk

- The amount of memory in your computer, along with the amount of memory currently unused by DOS

- An error message if damaged files exist

- All of the files on your disk (optional)

- Information about disk contiguity (optional)

The CHKDSK command can also recover damaged files for your examination.

Invoke CHKDSK simply by entering the command

[C:\] CHKDSK

CHKDSK will respond by displaying

Volume DOS 3-3   created Aug 2, 1988 1:52p

33439744 bytes total disk space
71680 bytes in 3 hidden files
10240 bytes in 3 directories
3024896 bytes in 211 user files
30332928 bytes available on disk

655360 bytes total memory
600272 bytes free

CHKDSK first displays the disk volume label and the date on which the volume label was assigned to the disk:

Volume DOS 3-3   created Aug 2, 1988 1:52p

Next, CHKDSK displays the total amount of information that your disk can store:

33439744 bytes total disk space

Each time you create a bootable DOS disk (with FORMAT /S), DOS creates on the disk two hidden system files that it uses during startup. Since these two files do not appear in your directory listings, they are called *hidden files*. (DOS will suppress the display of these files to prevent you from inadvertently deleting or renaming them.) When you assign a volume label to a disk, DOS creates a third hidden file. Note that all three files are listed in the CHKDSK output:

    71680 bytes in 3 hidden files

CHKDSK then displays the total number of subdirectories and files that reside on your hard disk:

    10240 bytes in 3 directories
    3024896 bytes in 211 user files

If the FORMAT command locates damaged locations on your disk, it marks them to prevent their use by DOS. If damaged sectors exist on your disk, CHKDSK will display the number of bytes of damaged disk space that the disk contains.

Next, CHKDSK displays the amount of available disk space:

    30332928   bytes available on disk

To determine how much disk space you are actually using, subtract this value from the total disk space that CHKDSK previously displayed:

    Space in use = total disk space - bytes available on disk
                 = 33,329,744 - 30,332,928
                 = 3,106,816 bytes

Finally, the CHKDSK command displays your current memory utilization:

```
655360 bytes total memory
600272 bytes free
```

The top number tells you the amount of memory present in your system, and the bottom number tells you amount of space that is currently in use by DOS.

It is not uncommon, during the everyday use of your disk, for files to become damaged due to such actions as restarting DOS or turning off your system while a program is running, or terminating a program with CTRL-BREAK. If this occurs, CHKDSK may display the message

```
nnn lost clusters found in n chains.
Convert lost chains to files (Y/N)?
```

To repair the damaged files, you must reinvoke CHKDSK and specify the /F qualifier, as shown here:

```
[C:\] CHKDSK /F
```

When CHKDSK later prompts

```
nnn lost clusters found in n chains.
Convert lost chains to files (Y/N)?
```

simply type **Y** and press ENTER. CHKDSK will copy all of the damaged files to the root directory of your disk, assigning them to files with the name FILE*nnnn*.CHK, as shown here:

```
Volume in drive C is DOS 3-3
Directory of  C:\
```

COMMAND	COM	37637	6-17-88	12:00p
WS	<DIR>		8-01-88	4:29p
CONFIG	SYS	22	8-01-88	4:41p
DOS	<DIR>		8-02-88	1:56p
FILE0000	CHK	8444	8-01-88	5:24p
FILE0001	CHK	2816	10-03-84	10:33p

6 File(s) 30300160 bytes free

By using the DOS TYPE command to display the file's contents, you may later be able to determine the file's contents and save information that might otherwise have been lost. At the worst, you can simply delete these files, freeing up the disk space that the file consumed.

If you include the /V qualifier in the CHKDSK command line, CHKDSK will display the name of each file and subdirectory on your disk:

[C:\] CHKDSK /V

▶ IMPROVING HARD-DISK RESPONSE TIME

Before you can access a file—either to read information from it or to write information to it—DOS must first verify that the file actually exists and can be opened as specified (remember, DOS will not allow you to open a read-only file for such activity as writing to it). If the file can be manipulated as requested, DOS allows the program to access the file. This process is called *opening* the file.

To determine this information, along with the starting location of the file on disk, DOS must read several pieces of information from your disk. Unfortunately, compared to the fast electronic speed of your computer, the mechanical disk-drive access (even for a hard disk) is slow. To reduce the amount of overhead associated with opening your commonly used files, DOS version 3.3 provides the FASTOPEN command.

Once you invoke FASTOPEN, DOS keeps the information (location on disk, access type, and so on) in memory for your most commonly used files. When DOS needs to access such a file later, all of the information DOS requires to open the file is already in memory. This, in turn, reduces the number of slow disk-drive I/O operations required, which improves your system performance. DOS version 3.3 provides FASTOPEN as an external command.

To keep track of your 30 most recently used files on drive C, for example, use the command

   [C:\] FASTOPEN C:=30

FASTOPEN allows you to track up to 999 files. However, if you specify too many files, you may actually decrease your system performance: FASTOPEN must then search a long list of files with each file-open operation, as well as consume considerable memory—each FASTOPEN entry consumes 40 bytes of memory. Most users should find a setting of 30 to 50 to be most efficient for their system. Remember, the goal of FASTOPEN is to reduce the amount of time it takes DOS to open your most commonly used files. Few of us have several hundred files that we open on a regular basis.

FASTOPEN only supports hard disks; since floppy disks can be removed, it doesn't make sense to track file locations. If you invoke FASTOPEN and specify a floppy-disk drive, FASTOPEN will fail and display

Cannot use FASTOPEN for drive A:

If your system has multiple hard-disk drives, FASTOPEN allows you to specify the number of files that DOS should track for each disk, as shown here:

[C:\] FASTOPEN C:=30 D:=30

If you specify several disks in this manner, the total number of file entries (for all of the disks) cannot exceed 999.

Finally, FASTOPEN installs memory-resident software when you invoke it. Therefore, you can only invoke FAST-OPEN once per user session. If you want to change your settings for FASTOPEN, you must first restart DOS.

▶ SAVING TIME AND KEYSTROKES

Users often type in much more information than DOS actually requires when they perform file-copying operations in conjunction with DOS subdirectories. For example, assume that you want to copy the FORMAT.COM file from the DOS subdirectory to the COMMANDS subdirectory. Many users will issue the command

[C:\]COPY \DOS\FORMAT.COM\ COMMANDS\FORMAT.COM
    1 File(s) copied

Although this command is quite readable, it contains more information than DOS needs. Since the name of the target file (FORMAT.COM) does not change from the source, DOS does not require you to include it in the command line. The following command is equivalent:

```
[C:\] COPY \DOS\FORMAT.COM \COMMANDS
        1 File(s) copied
```

When DOS encounters \COMMANDS, it will recognize that COMMANDS is the directory in which it should place the target file. Since a target file is not specified in the command line, DOS will use the same file name as the source file (FORMAT.COM) as desired.

Had the COMMANDS subdirectory been your current directory, you could have simply entered the command as:

```
[C:\COMMANDS] COPY \DOS\FORMAT.COM
        1 File(s) copied
```

Again, since no target file name is specified in the command line, DOS uses the same name as the source file. In this same way, if you wanted to copy all of the files from the DOS directory to the COMMANDS directory, you could enter the command

```
[C:\] COPY \DOS\*.* \COMMANDS\*.*
```

or

```
[C:\] COPY \DOS\*.* \COMMANDS
```

Finally, since DOS knows that the name DOS signifies a subdirectory, you can simply use

[C:\] COPY \DOS \COMMANDS

In any case, DOS will copy all of the files that reside in the DOS subdirectory to the COMMANDS subdirectory as desired. By knowing these simple tricks, you can save considerable typing.

► MAXIMIZING HARD-DISK PERFORMANCE

Speed is one of the major advantages of a hard disk. Since more and more people are spending considerable amounts of their day working with computers, getting the highest performance from the computer (and hence the hard disk) is always paramount. This section will take a look at several things that will help you maximize your hard disk's performance.

The CONFIG.SYS BUFFERS= entry allows you to reduce the number of disk input and output operations that DOS must perform. By reducing slow disk I/O operations, you can improve your system's performance. Here's why.

Because disk drives are mechanical, they are are inherently slow. To reduce the number of disk input/output operations that it must perform, DOS provides large storage regions in memory, called *disk buffers*. Each disk buffer can store 512 bytes of data, as shown here:

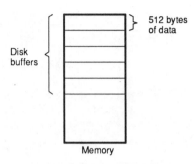

As you know, DOS divides your disks into storage regions called sectors as well. They are also 512 bytes in size.

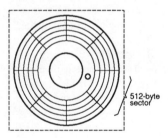

When DOS reads or writes information to disk, the smallest amount of information that DOS can transfer is 512 bytes. Assume, for example, that you have a payroll program that reads employee records containing a name, an address, the pay grade, and the number of dependents. Each record is 128 bytes in length:

Name	Address	Pay Grade	Dependents
Jones	1327 First St.	5	2
Kent	926 Downing	4	5
Lowry	1822 Fourth Ave.	4	1
Smith	173 Fifth St.	5	5
Wilson	19 Jones Dr.	7	3

When your program reads the first record in the file from disk, DOS must read 512 bytes (the disk sector size) from disk, as opposed to the 128 bytes that are required for the first record. DOS reads the 512 bytes into a disk buffer, and only returns the first 128 requested bytes to the program:

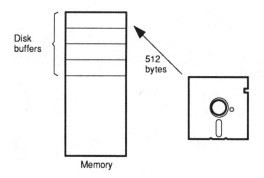

Disk buffers

512 bytes

Memory

Since DOS has read 512 bytes from disk with one read operation, reading data in this manner has the advantage that the next three records in the file now reside in memory instead of being on the slow disk. Thus, when your program later tells DOS to get the second record from the file, DOS doesn't have to read your disk—it already has the information in memory. This is true for the third and fourth records as well:

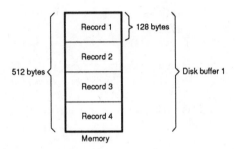

In this case, we have reduced the number of slow disk read operations by a factor of 4. Each time DOS must read information from disk, it actually performs the following processing steps:

- It checks to see if the information already resides in memory in a disk buffer. If the data is in a disk buffer, it uses it.

- If the data does not reside in memory, it reads the disk sector containing the data from disk into a disk buffer.

The BUFFERS= entry in CONFIG.SYS allows you to specify the number of buffers for which DOS provides space in memory each time your system boots. The format of this entry is

BUFFERS=*number_of_buffers*

where *number_of_buffers* can range from 2 to 255. Most users achieve best performance by using 20 to 25 buffers, as shown here:

    BUFFERS=25

If you make the number of buffers too large, you will use up considerable memory that DOS may need for other tasks, as well as creating a long list of buffers that DOS must examine each time it needs to read information from disk. For most applications, the value of 25 disk buffers is recommended.

DOS version 3.3 provides another method of maximizing your disk's speed: the FASTOPEN command. It directs DOS to track a specified number of the last files that you have accessed from your hard disk. If you are using DOS version 3.3, you might consider using a value of 30 to 50 for FASTOPEN:

    [C:\] FASTOPEN C:=30

As it turns out, your directory structure itself can have a considerable impact on your disk's performance. First of all, if your directories contain many files, DOS may spend a lot of time searching through the directory listing of files in order to locate a specific file. Subdividing your directories not only helps you organize your files, but it may also reduce long directory searches. Always keep in mind that disk I/O is slow; anything that you can do to reduce it will improve your system response time.

If you have an application that continually opens many different data files, the location at which you place the files in your subdirectory tree will influence your system's performance. For example, assume that you have a database program that maintains many files, and your directory structure is

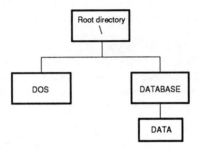

Each time your program accesses a file, DOS must first search the root directory to locate the DATABASE subdirectory, which requires disk I/O. Next, DOS must search the DATABASE subdirectory for the DATA subdirectory, which requires additional disk I/O operations. Finally, DOS must search the DATA subdirectory for the specific file, another set of I/O operations. All of this occurs before DOS can even open the specified file.

If your directory structure had instead been

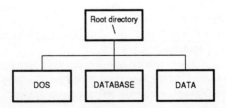

you would have eliminated the search of the DATABASE directory. In this case, DOS would locate the DATA directory within the root directory for the DATA subdirectory and then search that subdirectory for the specific file. Placing the DATA subdirectory below DATABASE makes very clear which application DATA applies to (DATA is associated with your database program, as opposed to your word processor or spreadsheet).

However, this increased file organization is not without cost. Your trade-off becomes speed of access versus file organization. However, you may like the additional disk organization that placing the DATA subdirectory below DATABASE provides.

If you are specifying several subdirectories within your command-file or data-file search paths (with the DOS PATH and APPEND commands), the order in which you specify subdirectory entries is critical to your response time. Always place the subdirectories that are most likely to contain your external commands or data files first in the appropriate path. For example, if you define a command-file search path as

[C:\] PATH C:\MISC;C:\GAMES;C:\DOS

then each time you invoke a DOS command, DOS must first search the MISC subdirectory and the GAMES subdirectory for the command before it begins looking in the DOS subdirectory. If these two subdirectories contain multiple files, DOS could spend considerable time performing needless search operations.

If a subdirectory is not likely to contain a command file, either place it last in the command-file search path or consider removing the subdirectory from the command completely.

Many third-party software vendors provide software that creates a *disk cache* (pronounced "cash") that is quite similar to DOS disk buffers but is on a larger scale. A disk-cache region can be much larger than the area supported by DOS disk buffers. In fact, if your system has several megabytes of memory (either extended or expanded memory), most caching programs will readily support all of it.

A disk cache contains more logic (intelligence) than does a DOS disk buffer. In fact, most disk caching programs can track the least- recently used buffer, make sure that disk output is immediately recorded to disk instead of being buffered in memory (called a write-through cache), and perform more optimal search operations for your data.

Disk caching works like DOS disk buffers in that, before DOS reads information from your disk, it checks the cache to see if the data already resides in memory. If the data resides in the cache, there is no reason to read it from disk. This, in turn, gives you better response time. For large database applications, the increase in performance can be quite impressive. Because the cache provides more optimal searches for your data, having a large cache does not affect your system performance as severely as a large number of DOS disk buffers might.

The only drawbacks to caching software is that you normally have to purchase additional third-party software, and very likely, additional memory. If you have a disk-intensive program, however, these additional expenses may be cost-effective. In the future, more and more manufacturers will provide caching software with their systems.

Earlier, you learned that DOS divides your disk into circular rings called cylinders. Within each cylinder, DOS further divides your disk into smaller pieces called segments.

Each of these segments can store 512 bytes (characters) of information.

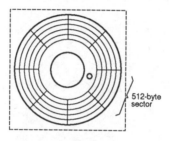

512-byte sector

When DOS reads or writes information to your disk, it does so by spinning your disk around in the drive rapidly in order to locate the desired segment. When your disks are new, DOS can store your files in consecutive, or *contiguous,* segments on disk, as shown here:

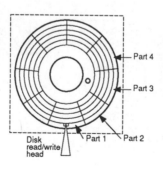

The advantage of having your disk stored in contiguous locations on disk is speed of access. In this case, once DOS reads the first part of the file, it needs to rotate the disk only a small distance in order to read the second part:

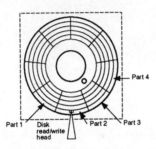

This process repeats for the third and fourth parts of the file, as shown here:

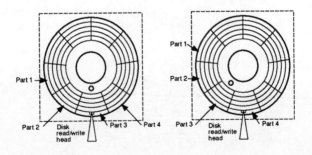

As you use your disks on a regular basis, DOS is no longer afforded the luxury of keeping your files in adjoining locations on disk. As you create and delete files, you make sectors available for storing information all over the disk. When it comes time for DOS to store your file, DOS must place the file on disk any where it will fit. As a result, portions of your file may end up widely dispersed about your disk:

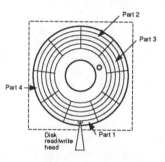

In this case, once DOS reads the first part of your file, it must rotate the disk a half a revolution in order to read part 2:

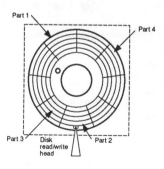

Next, to read part 3 of the file, your disk must rotate almost a complete revolution:

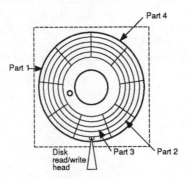

To read part 4 of the file requires one more partial rotation. As the size of your files increase, these additional disk rotations can become quite time-consuming.

CHKDSK gives you a tool for examining your disk. To examine a specific file for disk contiguity, simply type the file's name in the CHKDSK command line, as shown here:

```
A> CHKDSK DISKCOPY.COM
```

CHKDSK will display its standard information and then report on the file:

```
Volume MS330PP01 created Jul 24, 1988 11:28a
362496 bytes total disk space
```

```
53248 bytes in 3 hidden files
304128 bytes in 34 user files
5120 bytes available on disk

655360 bytes total memory
584544 bytes free
All specified file(s) are contiguous
```

If you want to examine your entire disk, use the DOS asterisk wildcard character:

```
A> CHKDSK B:*.*
```

If a file is noncontiguous, CHKDSK will display

```
C:\FILENAME.EXT
Contains n non-contiguous blocks
```

If your disk contains many files that are not contiguous, the only way to correct the problem is with a complete disk back-up, format, and restore operation as discussed later in this reference.

► BACKING UP YOUR HARD DISK

One of the most critical operations that you must perform on a regular basis is backing up your hard-disk files to floppy disks. The DOS BACKUP and RESTORE commands exist for one purpose—to help you prevent or reduce the loss of programs and data. You must perform backups on a regular basis; if you do not, DOS cannot prevent the loss of your data.

Before you examine the DOS BACKUP and RESTORE commands, you must do some preparatory work. First, you will need to know how many floppy disks your hard-disk backup will require. To determine the number of disks, first use CHKDSK to determine the total number of bytes currently in use:

```
[C:\] CHKDSK

21309440 bytes total disk space
53248 bytes in 2 hidden files
32768 bytes in 13 directories
6492160 bytes in 419 user files
69632 bytes in bad sectors
14661632 bytes available on disk

655360 bytes total memory
331536 bytes free

[C:\]
```

Next, use the following equation:

Number of disks = bytes in use /storage capacity
Bytes in use   = total disk space - bytes available
               = 21,309,440 - 14,661,632
               = 6,647,808 bytes

This table gives you a quick summary of your disk storage capabilities:

Disk Type	Storage capacity
Single-sided Double-density	184,320 bytes
Double-sided Double-density	368,640 bytes
Double-sided Double-density 3.5	737,280 bytes
Quad-density	1,228,800 bytes
High-capacity 3.5	1,474,560 bytes

Using a 360K floppy disk for an example, the equation becomes

$$\text{Number of disks} = 6,647,808/368,640$$
$$= 18.03$$
$$= 19 \text{ disks}$$

Using a 1.2 megabyte disk, produces

$$\text{Number of disks} = 6,647,808/1,228,800$$
$$= 5.41$$
$$= 6 \text{ disks}$$

Next, you need a way to store your floppy disks safely. A media storage box is recommended specifically for your backup disks:

If you have this box, should you ever need to restore a file from the backup disks, you will know exactly where your disks are.

Once you acquire a media storage box, find a safe location for it, preferably in a room other than the one containing your computer. Several sources of damage to your disk—such as smoke, theft, and spills—could also easily damage your backup disks if they were in the same room.

The goal of performing backups is to make duplicate copies of the files on your hard disk. Since most users will simply copy the files to floppy disk, all of the examples given here will use BACKUP to back up files from your hard disk to floppy disks in drive A.

In its most basic form, the DOS BACKUP command is

[C:\] BACKUP C:*.* A: /S

In this case, you are using BACKUP to back up the entire hard disk (C) to the floppy disks in drive A. The /S qualifier directs

BACKUP to include all of the files contained in DOS sub-directories. Note that a file specification is not included on the target drive, A; BACKUP only uses a disk-drive letter for the target drive.

BACKUP does not copy files to the target disk in the same manner as COPY or XCOPY. Instead, it uses a unique file format that allows it to keep track of files and subdirectories. Only BACKUP and RESTORE understand this file format. Once you create a backup floppy disk with BACKUP, the only way you can manipulate the files that it contains is with RESTORE. *Do not* try to copy the files. BACKUP places information at the front of each file that RESTORE later removes; if you simply copy the files, this header information will still be at the beginning of the file, making the file invalid.

BACKUP is a very powerful command that allows you to back up all of the files on your disk; a select group of files, based on the file's creation date and time; or just those files that you have created or modified since the last BACKUP command. Thus, the complete format of the BACKUP command

> BACKUP *source_files target_drive* [/S] [/M] [/A]
> [/F] [/D:*mm:dd:yy*] [/T:*hh:mm:ss*]
> [/L:*log_file_path*]

where the following definitions apply:

source_files specifies the files that BACKUP is to back up to your target drive.

target_drive is the disk-drive letter of the drive containing the floppy disk to which the files are to be copied.

/S directs BACKUP to also back up files contained in subdirectories.

/M directs BACKUP to back up only those files whose archive attribute is set in the file's attribute field.

/A adds the files to be backed up to those already on the target disk.

/F tells BACKUP to format each floppy disk before copying files to it.

/D:*mm:dd:yy* directs BACKUP to copy only files modified or created since the specified date.

/T:*hh:mm:ss* directs BACKUP to copy only files modified or created since the specified time.

/L:*log_file_path* directs BACKUP (under DOS version 3.3) to create a file that logs the backup disk on which each file is placed.

In most cases, you will want BACKUP to examine your entire disk to ensure that all of your files are backed up. However, you may often want BACKUP to back up only a specific file or a directory of files. Consider these examples. The first command directs BACKUP to back up all of the files in the DOS subdirectory:

    [C:\] BACKUP C:\DOS*.* A:

If all of the files in the subdirectory will not fit on the floppy disk in drive A, DOS will simply prompt

Insert backup diskette 02 in drive A:

Warning! Files in the target drive
A:\ root directory will be erased
Strike any key when ready

If this occurs, simply place a formatted disk in drive A and press ENTER to continue.

The BACKUP /F qualifier allows you to use an unformatted floppy disk for your BACKUP operations. If you specify the /F qualifier as in

[C:\] BACKUP C:*.* A: /S /F

BACKUP will format each disk that it uses during the backup operation. Although this seems very convenient, it slows down your backup process considerably. Therefore, whenever possible, format all of the floppy disks that you plan to use with BACKUP. Do not, however, format the disks as bootable system disks; this would use up a significant portion of the disk's storage capacity. Instead, simply use

[C:\] FORMAT A:

Before you can back up your entire hard disk to floppy disks, determine the number of disks that BACKUP will require as previously discussed. Next, assuming that the floppy disks are already formatted, issue the command

[C:\] BACKUP C:*.* A: /S

BACKUP will back up all of the files and subdirectories of files on your hard disk, C, to the floppy disk contained in drive A. Each time a floppy disk fills, BACKUP will display

Insert backup diskette *nn* in drive A:

Warning! Files in the target drive
A:\ root directory will be erased
Strike any key when ready

At that time, simply place a formatted disk in drive A and press ENTER. Make sure that you label each disk as BACKUP completes:

DRIVE C BACKUP — Backup type
09-12-88 — Backup date
DISK 1 of 22 — Disk number
KAJ — Person performing backup

Although the BACKUP command just shown allows you to back up your entire hard disk, to do so on a regular basis would be far too time-consuming. Instead, on the first day of each month, perform a complete backup of your disk with the command

110

[C:\] BACKUP C:*.* A: /S

Then, using a new set of disks, issue the following command each day for the remainder of the month:

[C:\] BACKUP C:*.* A: /S /A /M

This command directs BACKUP to back up only those files created that day (or since the last backup, which should have been the day before). You will end up with two sets of disks. The first set is your complete disk backup or monthly backup; the second is your daily backup disks.

Since you are backing up your files on a daily basis, it may take you several days, or even a week, to have enough files to fill up a floppy disk. Thus, using the /A qualifier, you can continue to use the same disk each day for daily backups until it becomes full and DOS displays

Insert backup diskette 02 in drive A:

Warning! Files in the target drive
A:\ root directory will be erased
Strike any key when ready

At that time, start using a second formatted disk, labeling the first and placing it in a safe location.

If you are using DOS version 3.3, BACKUP allows you to log which disk your files are stored on by means of the log-file directive /L. The contents of your log file will be as shown here:

```
[C:\] TYPE BACKUP.LOG

5-18-1988  14:19:36
001    \COMMAND.COM
001    \AUTOEXEC.BAT
001    \CONFIG.SYS
001    \DOS\COMMAND.COM
001    \DOS\ANSI.SYS
001    \DOS\COUNTRY.SYS
001    \DOS\DISPLAY.SYS
001    \DOS\DRIVER.SYS
001    \DOS\FASTOPEN.EXE
   .       .
   .       .
```

If you are using DOS version 3.3, create a subdirectory on
your hard disk called \BACKUP:

```
[C:\] MKDIR \BACKUP
```

When you invoke your monthly and daily BACKUP commands, include the /L qualifier, as shown here:

```
[C:\] BACKUP C:\*.* A: /S /L:C:\BACKUP\BACKUP.LOG
```

or

```
[C:\] BACKUP C:\*.* A: /S /A /M /L:C:\BACKUP\BACKUP.LOG
```

If you need to restore a file later, you can examine the log file
to determine on which disk the file resides.

The only way your backups will ever be helpful is if you perform them on a regular basis. The easiest way to do that is to create a backup policy and then to implement the policy with DOS batch files. You will need enough floppy disks to perform three complete hard-disk backups. Format each of these disks with

[C:\] FORMAT A:

Next, place the disks safely in a disk media storage box. On the first day of the month, issue the command

[C:\] BACKUP C:*.* A: /S

or the command

[C:\] BACKUP C:*.* A: /S /L:\BACKUP\BACKUP.LOG

if you are using DOS version 3.3. Label each disk. When BACKUP completes, place all of the disks in the media storage box.

As your next step, each day, using a set of daily backup disks (not monthly backup disks), issue either the command

[C:\] BACKUP C:*.* A: /S /A /M

or, if you are using DOS version 3.3,

[C:\] BACKUP C:*.* A: /S /A /M /L:\BACKUP\BACKUP.LOG

BACKUP will back up only those files created since your last backup. Continue to use the same floppy disk for your daily backups until it fills and DOS displays the message

Insert backup diskette 02 in drive A:

Warning! Files in the target drive
A:\ root directory will be erased
Strike any key when ready

At the first of the next month, use your unused floppy disks to perform a complete disk backup. If this backup is successful, you can recycle the previous monthly and daily backup disks.

▶ ACCESSING FILES ON A BACKUP FLOPPY DISK

The only way to access files contained on a backup floppy disk is with the DOS RESTORE command. If you delete a file inadvertently or a file becomes damaged, use the log file that BACKUP created to locate the disk containing your file:

A> PRINT C:\BACKUP\BACKUP.LOG

Inserting the correct disk into drive A, type the command

[C:\] RESTORE A: C:\PATHNAME\FILENAME.EXT

Consider these examples. The following command restores the LABEL.COM file to the DOS subdirectory.

[C:\] RESTORE A: C:\DOS\LABEL.COM

This command restores all of the files in your EXPENSES subdirectory:

    [C:\] RESTORE A: C:\EXPENSES*.*

If EXPENSES contains additional DOS subdirectories, add
the /S qualifier as shown here:

    [C:\] RESTORE A: C:\EXPENSES*.* /S

To restore your entire hard disk, your RESTORE command
becomes

    [C:\] RESTORE A: C:*.* /S

RESTORE will not restore the hidden DOS system files.
The complete format of the DOS RESTORE command is

    RESTORE *source_drive:*
    target_drive:file_specification [/S]
    [/P] [/A:*mm:dd:yy*] [/B:*mm:dd:yy*] [/E:*hh:mm:ss*]
    [/L:*hh:mm:ss*] [/M] [/N]

where the following definitions apply:

    source_drive is the drive letter of the floppy-disk drive
that contains the backup disk.
    target_drive:file_specification specifies the files that
RESTORE is to restore from floppy.
    /S directs RESTORE to also restore DOS subdirectories.
    /P directs RESTORE to pause, requesting permission to
restore files that have been marked read-only on your hard
disk.

115

/A:*mm:dd:yy* directs RESTORE to restore only those files modified or created after the specified date.

/B:*mm:dd:yy* directs RESTORE to restore only those files modified or created before the specified date.

/E:*hh:mm:ss* directs RESTORE to restore only those files modified or created before the specified time.

/L:*hh:mm:ss* directs RESTORE to restore only those files modified or created after the specified time.

/M directs RESTORE to restore only those files modified since the last backup.

/N directs RESTORE to restore only those files that no longer exist on your hard disk.

► UPGRADING TO A NEW VERSION OF DOS

Many hard disk users put off installing a new version of DOS simply because they do not understand the steps involved. As you will see here, upgrading DOS on your hard disk is quite straightforward.

First, place the DOS Programs disk for the new version of DOS in drive A and reboot. Once the new version of DOS is active, run all of the applications that you use on a daily basis to ensure that each still works. If one of your critical applications does not work, contact your dealer or software developer before continuing with the upgrade. In some cases, you may need to place a CONFIG.SYS file on the new DOS disk that contains the entry

```
FILES=20
```

before your application can work successfully.

Remember, by default, DOS only allows your application to open three files.

Next, with your DOS disk still in drive A, issue the command

A> SYS C:

The DOS SYS command transfers to your hard disk the hidden files that DOS requires to boot the new version of DOS. If DOS displays the message

System transferred

you are almost done; skip the next few paragraphs to the discussion of the DOS ATTRIB command. If, instead, DOS displays the message

No room for system on destination disk

you are going to have to perform the installation the hard way, by first backing up your disk as shown here:

A> BACKUP C:*.* A: /S

When the BACKUP command completes, you will now have to format your hard disk. Only issue the FORMAT command if your BACKUP command completed successfully:

A> FORMAT C: /S

Once your disk is formatted, you must restore all of the files that you just copied from your hard disk:

```
A> RESTORE  A:  C:\*.*  /S
```

Next, you must set all of your DOS files to read/write access with ATTRIB, as shown here:

```
A> ATTRIB  -R  C:\DOS\*.*
```

When this command completes, you can copy your new DOS commands to your hard disk. Begin with the COMMAND.COM file:

```
A> COPY  COMMAND.COM  C:\
```

Next, copy all of the files from your DOS disks into the DOS subdirectory:

```
A> COPY  *.*  C:\DOS
```

Remove the disk from drive A and restart DOS. Your hard-disk upgrade is now complete.

▶ USING A TAPE BACKUP SYSTEM

Until recently, the cost of installing a tape backup system in a computer reduced their popularity. However, a tape backup system can be quite convenient. It looks like this:

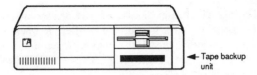

◄— Tape backup
unit

The advantages of a tape backup system are speed and ease of use. As you have seen, floppy-disk backups require constant interaction and many disks. Most tape backup systems use a technology called *streaming,* which allows them to back up a 20-megabyte disk in around 30 minutes, unattended! Many businesses will find tape backup systems to be cost-effective investments.

To discuss all of the different features that tape backup systems provide would require a second pocket reference, so this reference will offer only a few tips. If you are considering a tape backup system, make sure that you purchase a tape system that can store at least as much information as your hard disk. Ideally, you want a system capable of storing one and a half to two times as much information. Many tape systems provide software that allows you to perform monthly and daily backups. If your tape system is larger than your disk, you can place both the disk and incremental file backups on the same tape.

If you are comparing systems—and you should—make sure that the dealers are all using the same type of comparison. Depending upon the type of backup operation the system is performing, the speed of the backup will vary accordingly. In order to have a "standard" unit of measure, have the dealer perform a complete file-by-file backup of a disk of your size, with verification enabled. Obtain a count of the actual number of files backed up. This is the most time-consuming back-up operation, but it is also the most flexible when restore operations are required. If all of the dealers perform this back-up, you will have a better performance indicator for each of the systems.

▶ THIRD-PARTY BACKUP SOFTWARE

If you find that you are spending a considerable amount of time on your disk backups or that you aren't doing them because BACKUP and RESTORE are too complex, many third-party software developers provide menu-driven backup programs that are designed to give you the best performance. Simply contact your computer retailer for specifics on each system.

▶ REPAIRING A FRAGMENTED DISK

As you learned earlier in this reference, through the daily creation and deletion of files, your disks can become fragmented, which decreases their performance. At that time you learned the only means DOS provides to repair a fragmented disk is by performing a backup, format, and restore operation. If CHKDSK informs you that the majority of your files are fragmented, make a complete backup of your hard disk with the command

    [C:\] BACKUP C:*.* A: /S

Next, if the BACKUP command successfully completes, format your hard disk:

    [A:\] FORMAT C: /S

Once the FORMAT command completes, restore the files to your disk:

    [A:\] RESTORE A: C:*.* /S

CHKDSK should tell you that your disk is now contiguous.

▶ RECOMMENDATIONS FOR CONFIG.SYS

Each time DOS starts, it searches the root directory of your boot device for a file called CONFIG.SYS. If this file is in the root directory, DOS uses the entries that it contains to configure itself in memory. Several CONFIG.SYS entries directly influence your hard-disk capabilities, so you should make sure that the root directory of your hard disk contains this file and that you use the values specified here as your guidelines for the entries CONFIG.SYS contains.

As you learned earlier, the DOS BUFFERS= entry allows you to specify the number of DOS disk buffers that DOS creates when your system boots. By increasing the number of disk buffers, it is possible for you to reduce the number of disk I/O operations that DOS must perform. For most applications, a value of 25 disk buffers will be optimal:

BUFFERS=25

Each time DOS starts, it sets aside enough space for your programs to open eight files. Unfortunately, DOS predefines five of these files for the use of hardware devices attached to your computer. Thus, by default, your applications are restricted to opening only three files at a time. For most programs, this is unacceptable.

The DOS FILES= entry allows you to define the number of files that DOS will support. In most cases, a value of 20 should be sufficient:

FILES=20

DOS allows you to specify up to 250 files for this entry; however, each file entry consumes additional memory. Since you probably will never need more than 20 files open at a time, specifying more than 20 simply wastes memory.

If you will be installing DOS device drivers (such as ANSI.SYS) each time DOS starts, DOS allows you to keep the files in DOS subdirectories. To do so, simply precede the device-driver name with the corresponding subdirectory within your DEVICE= entry, as shown here:

DEVICE=C:\DOS\ANSI.SYS

Finally, if you wish to remove the COMMAND.COM file from your root directory, leaving the file in the DOS subdirectory, the SHELL= entry allows you to do just that. Simply specify the complete path name to COMMAND.COM, including the /P qualifier as shown here:

```
SHELL=C:\DOS\COMMAND.COM /P
```

If you do not include the /P qualifier, DOS will not execute the AUTOEXEC.BAT file, nor display the DATE and TIME commands.

A sample CONFIG.SYS file might contain the following:

```
[C:\] COPY CON \CONFIG.SYS
FILES=20
BUFFERS=25
^Z
        1 File(s) copied

[C:\]
```

▶ RECOMMENDATIONS FOR AUTOEXEC.BAT

Each time DOS starts, it searches the root directory of your boot device for a batch file named AUTOEXEC.BAT. If DOS locates this file, it executes all of the commands that the file contains. If the file does not exist, DOS displays the familiar DATE and TIME commands.

The first command that you place in your AUTO-EXEC.BAT file should be the DOS PATH command, which allows you to define your command-file search path. At a minimum, your PATH entry should contain

```
PATH=C:\DOS
```

Next, to help you keep better track of your current directory, define your DOS prompt to contain the current disk drive and subdirectory, as discussed earlier in this reference:

PROMPT [$p]

If you want to define a data-file search path with APPEND, specify the desired subdirectory entries as shown here:

APPEND C:\DATA /X

Not all DOS commands support data file search paths by default. If you include the /X qualifier, you increase the number of applications that support APPEND.

If you are using DOS version 3.3 or later, you might want to consider placing the FASTOPEN command in your AUTOEXEC.BAT file to decrease the amount of time that DOS spends searching for your commonly used files:

FASTOPEN C:=30

Finally, if you have used the SHELL= entry to move the COMMAND.COM file from your root directory to a DOS subdirectory, you will need to use the DOS SET command to modify the COMSPEC= entry in the DOS environment to reference the same location that you specified in your SHELL= entry, as shown here:

SET COMSPEC=C:\DOS\COMMAND.COM

The following illustrates a sample AUTOEXEC.BAT file:

```
[C:\] COPY CON \AUTOEXEC.BAT
PATH C:\DOS
PROMPT [$p]
FASTOPEN C:=30
^Z
    1 File(s) copied
```

► CARING FOR YOUR HARD DISK

Although your hard disk is built into your computer's chassis and its internal components are somewhat protected, your hard disk is still susceptible to many of the dangers that plague floppy disks. First of all, because your hard disk is much more precise than a floppy disk, even the smallest pieces of dust or particles of smoke can damage the disk. As you know, information is recorded to and from your disk by means of the disk drive's read/write head. This head sits very close to your disk's surface, but it should not make contact with the disk. When it does, it will probably scratch the recording surface of the disk and your disk will be severely damaged. Such an occurrence is called a *head crash*.

If you take care of your computer, keeping your room dust- and smoke-free, the likelihood of a head crash is rare. Keep in mind, however, how smoke and dust particles compare in size to the separation between your disk drive's read/write head and the disk itself:

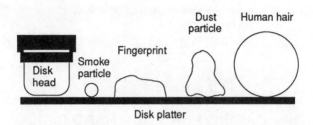

Disk platter

Should there be a dust or smoke particle on your disk, it could easily cause a head crash. Always keep your computer as free of dust and smoke as you can. In today's office environments, this is not always an easy task.

Moving your disk roughly can also cause a head crash. Disks are sensitive devices; treat them as such. As you work with your disk, keep the following rules in mind:

- Never allow magnetic or powerful electronic devices other than your computer near your disk. They could erase the information magnetically recorded on your disk.

- Never place your telephone near your hard disk. Each time your phone rings, it produces a powerful electronic flux that could erase information recorded on your disk.

- Disks are sensitive to temperature. Never let your disks get too hot or too cold. Keep your disks out of direct sunlight.

- Don't smoke near your disk, since even the smallest smoke or dust particle can damage your disk. If

possible, don't allow smoking in the same room as
your computer.

* Always move your computer with care.

▶ MOVING YOUR SYSTEM

Your hard disk needs to be handled gently to prevent a disk
head crash. However, if you are moving your computer from
one location to another, you have to expect some movement.
Most hard disks provide a designated landing zone on which
the disk head can be parked when you move your system:

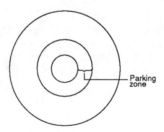

Parking
zone

By parking your disk head in this manner, you reduce the risk
of damaging your disk during the move.

Some systems automatically park the head each time you
turn your system off. Other systems provide software that
parks the head. In the case of the IBM PC AT, for example,
the Setup program provided in the "Guide to Operations"

manual allows you to prepare your disk for moving as shown
here:

> SELECT AN OPTION
>
> 0 - SYSTEM CHECKOUT
> 1 - FORMAT DISKETTE
> 2 - COPY DISKETTE
> 3 - PREPARE SYSTEM FOR MOVING
> 4 - SETUP
> 9 - END DIAGNOSTICS
>
> SELECT THE ACTION DESIRED
> ?

When you later turn your computer's power back on, the disk
head will leave the parking zone as desired.